Tazkiyah

THE ISLAMIC PATH OF SELF-DEVELOPMENT

Tazkiyah

THE ISLAMIC PATH OF
SELF-DEVELOPMENT

Edited by Abdur Rashid Siddiqui

THE ISLAMIC FOUNDATION

Published by

THE ISLAMIC FOUNDATION

Markfield Conference Centre, Ratby Lane,
Markfield, Leicestershire, LE67 9SY, United Kingdom
Tel: (01530) 244944/5, Fax: (01530) 244946
E-mail: info@islamic-foundation.org.uk
E-mail: publications@islamic-foundation.org.uk
Website: www.islamic-foundation.org.uk

Quran House, PO Box 30611, Nairobi, Kenya

PMB, 3193, Kano, Nigeria

British Library Cataloguing-in-Publication Data

Tazkiyah: the Islamic path of self-development
1.Religious life - Islam 2.Muslims - Conduct of life
I.Siddiqui, A. R. (Abdur Rashid), 1932-
297.5'7

ISBN 0 86037 349 5

Typeset and Cover design: Nasir Cadir
Printed and bound in Great Britain by Antony Rowe Ltd, Chippenham, Wiltshire

Contents

Preface

The term self-development is used in many disciplines both scientific and religious. In business management it denotes managers' self-understanding and ability to recognize their strengths and offset their weaknesses, thus developing their potentialities for success in enterprise. Self-development as understood by mystics and Sufis signifies self-purification from all bad traits and habits and devotion to the worship of God, cutting oneself off from worldly affairs and leading a pious life in order to achieve gnosis of some other kind or degree of union with God.

However, orthodox Islamic teaching about self-development is quite different from the above two concepts. According to the Qur'ān and the *Sunnah* piety is not running away from the problems of life, nor is it attainment of union with God. Worldly success is also desirable but felicity in the Hereafter is the final goal. Obedience to Allah in all affairs of one's life is the zenith of self-development. It demands spiritual development but also entails that one tries to lead a balanced life looking after one's family, reforming society and being an active and sincere citizen.

Those working for the revival of Islam in our times recognize that self-development lies at the core of their striving. Their success in this life and the next depends very much on it. They therefore believe that self-development should be pursued as a conscious, systematic exercise.

There are many works in Islamic literature on the subject of self-development, written from a variety of angles. Apart from *tafāsīr* and commentaries on *aḥādīth*, there are many books and articles expressly dedicated to this subject. Whoever embraces Islam now or is a Muslim inevitably passes through the stages of training, self-development and self-purification. But unfortunately there are hardly any books in English that cover self-development from an authentic Islamic perspective. This anthology has been compiled to meet that need, by translating works that originally appeared in Urdu. Some contributions are from leaders of the Islamic Movement of the last century.

In a collection of this sort overlap and repetition are inevitable to some degree. However each contributor has his own style and way of elucidation of the concept from different angles. Mawlānā Mawdūdī (may Allah have mercy on him) has illustrated the difference between the Islamic way of self-development and others by using the vivid simile of arms manufacture. His contribution also includes discussion of the qualities for self-development and the pitfalls to be avoided.

Mawlānā Fāruq Khān in his work as well as discussing self-development also brings out the importance and relevance of morals and motivation. It is therefore hoped that study of this essay will help allay doubts and misconceptions. The main point emphasized is that the Qur'ānic directives on constructing an Islamic society are perfectly in harmony with the human nature and free from any imbalance.

Ustādh Khurram Murad (may Allah's Mercy be upon him) has taken a very frank and direct approach to self-development. According to him, 'Self-development is attainable only by taking control of one's life and by personal initiative. It cannot be gained simply by studying books, listening to lectures and sermons, attending training courses and programmes and keeping the company of elders and righteous people. For it is a law of nature that none can do for you what you are obliged to do. Of course self-development is not possible without the ability and guidance provided by Allah. However, even this can be earned by one's own efforts.' Thus he provides a practical guide clarifying the straight way leading to self-purification and self-development. It is a compact code of conduct that will help the individual to develop himself.

Mawlānā Amīn Aḥsan Iṣlāḥī's work (may Allah have mercy on him) deals with self-development in the context of man's relationship with Allah and with his own self, as these are stated in the Qur'ān and the *Sunnah* and to clarify the prerequisites and other implications of these obligations.

In my own contribution I have raised the question whether self-development can really be left to happen by itself, or if deliberate efforts should be made to achieve it. As a worker for the revival of Islam in modern times I recognize that self-development lies at the core of our struggle. Therefore I believe that self-development should be pursued deliberately and systematically. Efforts should be made to incorporate techniques and methods appropriate to the challenges of modern times.

I gratefully acknowledge and thank the following publishers whose publications we have translated into English in this book: Markazī Maktabah Islāmī, Delhi for the contributions of Sayyid Abu'l A'lā Mawdūdī, Mawlānā Muḥammad Fārūq and Mawlānā Amīn Aḥsan Iṣlāḥī and Manshūrāt, Lahore for the contributions of Abdur Rashid Siddiqui and Ustādh Khurram Murad.

My grateful thanks are due to Dr. Jamil Qureshi for his editorial help. I am also indebted to my friend and colleague Dr. Manazir Ahsan for checking diacritical markings as well as making very valuable suggestions. I am also grateful to him for agreeing to publish this work from the Islamic Foundation. I take this opportunity to thank Mr. Naiem Qaddoura and Mr. Nasir Cadir for their indispensable help in the production of this book. May Allah reward them all for their selfless efforts. *Amin*

May Allah make this book a means to help its readers and to infuse in them a sense of responsibility and accountability. All praise belongs to Allah, the Lord of the worlds.

Leicester,   **Abdur Rashid Siddiqui**
August 2003

Biographical Notes

Amīn Aḥsan Iṣlāḥī (1904-1997)

Mawlānā Amīn Aḥsan Iṣlāḥī was one of the leading scholars of the Indian sub-continent. He graduated from the Madrasa al-Islāh, Azamgarh, India, an enlightened institution established by Mawlānā Shiblī Nuʿmānī. He was greatly influenced and inspired by an eminent *mufassir*, Mawlānā Ḥamiduddīn Farāhī. Together they established a methodology of understanding the Qur'ān by giving primacy to its *naẓm* (coherence and order) and the logical arrangement of verses and *sūrahs*. He joined the Jamāʿat-e-Islāmī at its inception in 1942 and was a leading personality in pioneering the Islamic movement in its early stages. He later disagreed with the strategy of *daʿwah* and participation in elections in Pakistan and withdrew from the Jamāʿat.

His *magnum opus* is the 9-volume commentary in Urdu entitled *Tadabbur-e-Qur'ān*. Some of his important works are *Daʿwat-e-Dīn awr us kā Ṭarīqah-i-Kār* (The Call to Islam and

How to Invite Others to Islam, *Tazkiyah-e-Nafs* (Self-development and Purification of the Soul), *Mabādī Tadabbur-e-Qur'ān* (Principles of Pondering Over the Qur'ān) and Islamic State series pamphlets. His eloquent speeches and writings on *da'wah*, Islamic state and many other topics has inspired generations of young Muslims. He also had studied the *Ḥadīth* in depth. His lectures on *Ṣaḥīḥ al-Bukhārī* and *Muwwaṭṭa' Imām Mālik* are collected and are being published by Idārah Tadabbur-e-Qur'ān wa Ḥadīth, Lahore which he established.

Muḥammad Fārūq Khān (1932-)

Mawlānā Muḥammad Fārūq Khān was born in 1932 in Karpi, District Sultanpur, India. He did his postgraduate degree in Hindi language and learned Arabic under several learned scholars so that he could study the Qur'ān, *Ḥadīth* and Islamic Thought in depth. He started his career as a teacher of Islamic Studies and then engaged in writing. Being a scholar of Sanskrit and Hindi he translated the Qur'ān into Hindi language and published a two-volume collection of *aḥādīth* entitled *Kalām-e-Nabūwat* both in Hindi and Urdu, each with short explanations. He also translated the Urdu work of Mawlānā Mawdūdī, *Tafhīm al-Qur'ān* as well as several other important Arabic and Urdu books in Hindi. He is the author of over 30 books on Islam, Islamic thought and particularly Islam and Hinduism. He has developed a deep interest in both Urdu and Hindi poetry and literature. Collections of his poetical compositions in both languages are highly acclaimed.

Sayyid Abu'l A'lā Mawdūdī (1903-1979)

Sayyid Mawdūdī was the most eminent Islamic thinker, reformer and scholar of the last century. His thought has spread all over the world and greatly influenced the work of Islamic *da'wah*. He was a prolific writer and has written in an extremely lucid and logical style on most topics that needed guidance for the revival of Islam. He explained the Islamic teachings to solve the problems faced by the *ummah* in the 20th century.

He was the founder of Jamā'at-e-Islāmī and made an indelible mark on history by organizing a successful Islamic movement and leading it through different turbulent periods. Among his major works are *Tafhīm al-Qur'ān* (Towards Understanding the Qur'ān) in six volumes, *Sūd* (Usury) in two volumes, *Ma'āshiyāt-e-Islāmī* (The Islamic Economics), *Islāmī Riyāsat* (The Islamic State) *al-Jihād fil-Islām* (*Jihād* in Islam) and *Pardah* (Veil). He wrote many articles on the critique of the Western thought and strategy of Islamic *da'wah* which were published in the journal he started in 1932 called *Tarjumān al-Qur'ān*. He was a man of tremendous courage and insight and has left a lasting legacy of Islamic *da'wah* work around the world.

Khurram Murad (1932-1996)

Ustādh Khurram Murad studied civil engineering at the universities of Karachi, Pakistan and Minnesota, USA, and worked as a consulting engineer at Karachi, Dhaka, Tehran and in Saudi Arabia. He was actively involved in the Islamic movement since his student days. He was the President of Islāmī Jamī'at-e-Ṭalabah, Pakistan

(1951-52); a member of the Central Executive, Jamā'at-e-Islāmī Pakistan (1963-96) and Amīr of its Dhaka and Lahore branches. He held the post of Nā'ib Amīr of Jamā'at (1988-96).

He was actively involved in the training of Islamic workers and his engaging personality inspired countless young persons to take up the challege of *da'wah* work. His year-long training programmes for young people resulted in the formation of Young Muslims UK. His *Dars-e-Qur'ān* and moving lectures changed the thinking and lifestyle of countless people.

He was appointed the editor of the prestigious journal *Tarjumān al-Qur'ān* in 1991 and he continued to edit it until his death in 1996. His translations of Mawlānā Mawdūdī's books into English have captured the exuberance of Mawdūdī's style. His guide to the study of the Qur'ān entitled *The Way to the Qur'ān* is acclaimed as one of the best books on this subject in English. Many of his books both in English and Urdu are being published posthumously.

Abdur Rashid Siddiqui (1932-)

Abdur Rashid Siddiqui gained an honours degree in Economics and Politics from the University of Bombay and has a law degree from the same University. He completed his postgraduate study in Librarianship in London and was elected an Associate of the Library Association. He worked as an Information Librarian at the University of Leicester from 1966 until his retirement in 1997.

He has been deeply involved in Islamic activities for many years. He was one of the earliest members of the UK Islamic Mission and is a member of its *Shūrā*. He was one of the founder members of the Islamic Society of Britain and was the Chairman of its *Shūrā* Council for many years. He is the Secretary of the Board of Trustees of the Islamic Foundation, UK.

His publications are *Lift Up Your Hearts: A collection of 30 Khuṭbahs for Friday prayers*; *Key to al-Fātiḥah: Understanding the Basic Concepts*; *Key to Āl 'Imrān: Resurgence of the Ummah* and *Nawā-e-Benawā* (an anthology of Urdu poetry). He has also contributed a number of articles on a variety of subjects.

Transliteration Table

Consonants. Arabic

initial: unexpressed medial and final:

ء	ʾ	د	d	ض	ḍ	ك	k
ب	b	ذ	dh	ط	ṭ	ل	l
ت	t	ر	r	ظ	ẓ	م	m
ث	th	ز	z	ع	ʿ	ن	n
ج	j	س	s	غ	gh	ھـ	h
ح	ḥ	ش	sh	ف	f	و	w
خ	kh	ص	ṣ	ق	q	ي	y

Vowels, diphthongs, etc.

Short:	ـَ	a	ـِ	i	ـُ u
long:	ـَا	ā	ـِي	ī	ـُو ū
diphthongs:			ـَوْ	aw	
			ـَىْ	ay	

CHAPTER I

The Islamic Concept of Self-development

Sayyid Abu'l A'lā Mawdūdī

SELF-DEVELOPMENT AND THE ROLE OF SOCIETY

In the Islamic scheme of things the growth of an individual's character and bringing it to perfection is a goal in itself. Islam addresses individuals, requiring them to worship and obey Allah. It charges them with responsibilities and obligations; it requires them to observe the lawful and the unlawful. Reward is promised to them for their adherence to faith and dire warnings are served to them for disobedience. In the Islamic perspective the individual is seen as the main player in the overall action. As a doer every individual will be duly recompensed. Islam therefore appeals to an individual's reason and emotions and directs its guidance to him. It seeks his felicity and protects him against loss and suffering. If the individual's conduct is defective, his association with a group or society cannot deliver him. On the contrary, his link with a pious group will be used as a strong argument against him for his failure in having made the best use of the opportunities available to him. It will aggravate his crime. By contrast, if he reaches the highest point possible in his self-development and develops his character as much as he can, the general decadence in his society cannot obstruct his deliverance and felicity. Rather, he will be credited for his positive efforts in a hostile atmosphere. This point is eloquently made in the Qur'ān thus: 'On you rests the case of yourselves; it cannot harm you as long as you keep yourselves guided.' (al-Mā'idah 5:105)

The Individual and Society

The above account does not imply that Islam pays no regard to social reform. It is of the utmost importance, but it is not a goal by itself. Since the growth of an individual's character and the full blossoming of his potentials are contingent upon the well-being of society, it may be regarded as desirable that the collective life too should be sound and morally upright. Human beings are no doubt born as individuals. However, they cannot lead life only as individuals. Even prior to his birth an individual assimilates the traits of his society as embodied by his parents. He inherits much from his parents, and that has an important bearing on the growth and development of his character. Society exercises its impact upon him from cradle to grave. If the collective life is built on wrong principles and is conducive to perpetrating crimes and sins and to promoting evil, it will be hard for most individuals to attain self-development to any degree. At times, the conditions are so adverse that even an outstanding Messenger feels constrained to exclaim: 'And Noah said: "Lord! Leave not of the infidels any inhabitant upon earth. For should You leave them, they will lead astray Your bondmen and will surely beget sinning infidels."' (Nūḥ 71:26-27)

It is therefore necessary that society be set right and collective life conform to sound beliefs. This in turn, will facilitate self-development and individuals will grow into good human beings. It is not possible for one to earn a livelihood through lawful means if the whole economy is controlled by un-Islamic forces. The Prophet (peace and blessings be upon him) is on record as declaring that one who has subsisted on unlawful earnings will be barred from entering Paradise and that he will be hurled into Hellfire. The *Jāhilīyah* order (ignorance), its morals and thought patterns, entail eternal loss and suffering for man. How can one escape its evil effect, if the *Jāhilīyah* order dominates social relations, education and other walks of life? Like poison it affects the whole fabric of life. One cannot attain any self-development or perfection if he is guilty of disobeying Allah and His Messenger. One is compelled into disregarding Allah and His Messenger if the political system is annexed by unbelievers and they coerce entire communities into committing injustice and corruption. In such an event an individual cannot work for his deliverance. Rather, it is essential for his success that all those obstacles to his growth and development be removed that are born of a degenerate social system. It should be replaced with a sound, pious collective life, which facilitates the individual's growth and development.

Collective life – an individual's testing ground

In a sense the way to one's self-development passes through collective life. It cannot be achieved in isolation from it. The individual must prove his mettle through social relations, his success or failure in the next life depends upon it. He cannot retire to a wilderness, forsaking the challenges of life. His role consists very much in performing his obligations towards others. He cannot survive on his own. On the contrary, he is tied by many bonds to others – as someone's son, father, brother, husband, friend or enemy, neighbour, employer or employee, superior or subordinate, trustee or dependent. His test consists in fulfilling his obligations as prescribed by Allah while he is bound to many by a number of ties. He is expected to play his role amidst fear and expectation, love and anger, hope and despair while he is burdened with trusts and responsibilities. It is to be seen how far he adheres to the limits set by Allah and how he discharges his role as His vicegerent. He is also tested as to what qualities he develops, what traits he displays and what legacy he leaves behind for his heirs. The Islamic concept of virtue loses all its meaning if an individual severs his ties with collective, social life. If the individual takes up fewer responsibilities, he hardly undergoes any test and fails to develop his character. One who opts for the renunciation of life and lives as an ascetic abandons the test altogether in neglecting the opportunities available to him for his self-development. He will not, of course, get any credit for his inaction and lassitude.

Not only does an individual get a chance to develop his character in collective life; he is able to discharge many of his obligations towards Allah only if he plays an active role in social life. If a pious person refuses power and authority, he cannot perform most of his obligations towards Allah. For, if rebels against Allah assume power and have control over culture, politics and economy, it might result in the suspension of *Sharī'ah* commands. Corruption will overwhelm social life. Far from enjoining good and forbidding evil, people will rather promote vices and suppress virtues. This is detestable in the sight of Allah. There is no realistic chance that one's spiritual exercises or nominal preaching of Islam, which may not offend unbelievers, will lead to any fruitful result. The only way to self-development consists in removing ungodly persons from positions of power and authority and in devoting one's total energy and resources to upholding and enforcing *Sharī'ah* in the land, which will put an end to mischief and corruption, promote virtue and piety while forbidding evil.

What Islam demands of an individual

As is evident from the foregoing, collective life has an important bearing on an individual. Nevertheless, pride of place belongs to the individual, since social reform or extirpation of social evils is geared only towards the goal of training pious individuals.

Of all the faiths, Islam places the greatest emphasis on an individual's reform and self-development. Islam nonetheless differs radically from faiths that focus only on individuals in isolation from social context. Such faiths are concerned only with personal spiritual development at the expense of neglecting social life. Equally, Islam has nothing in common with those systems that disregard individual persons and regard them merely as members of the group. These train individuals for a particular cause. The

Islamic stance on this issue holds the middle ground: it proclaims that every individual is answerable to Allah in his personal capacity, but this answerability is mostly about his social obligations and role. His ultimate success depends on collective reform. One cannot truly attain Allah's pleasure unless he seeks, to the extent possible, to eradicate injustice and corruption and establish divine commands on earth. Man stands charged with this responsibility as Allah's vicegerent. An individual, therefore, should not be concerned only with his own reform. Rather, he should equip himself to fight against the un-Islamic order and strive for the establishment of a pious social order.

Owing to centuries of decline many changes have crept into Muslim thinking. Their concept of self-development now is very different from what it was originally. The concept has become too narrow and the ways and means for attaining it have also undergone a substantial change. Things are not as they were in the Prophet's day. There are, no doubt, institutions for the purpose of achieving self-development. However, notwithstanding their presence, the *Jāhilīyah* order has established its domination all over the world, including Muslim lands and in fields as varied as literature, martial arts, scholarship, culture and civilization. Certain factors account for it and we should not feel shy of admitting this bitter truth.

For many Muslims the objective of self-development has been to attain truth by way of seeing directly the ultimate reality which indeed belongs to the realm of the Unseen. This is no doubt a lofty objective. However, the Qur'ān does not ask us to pursue that objective by devoting ourselves to it heart and soul. Even if we consider it as the ideal, according to the

Qur'ān, it can be attained only by a Messenger. Allah alone knows the truth related to the Unseen and He divulges part of it to only a Messenger of His choice, who is escorted by guardian angels. This arrangement is devised in order to ascertain whether the Messenger conveys faithfully the divine message. Allah has provided man with the requisite knowledge of the realm of the Unseen through His Messengers. It stands out as a major divine favour. For it has saved man from great hardship in finding out these truths on his own. Man is asked to believe in the message delivered by Messengers and perform his duties, without making any effort to perceive the Unseen.

Some misconstrue self-development in the sense of only personal spiritual growth. This has an occult side which one cannot fathom even after life-long study. The terminology and allusions used in this context are so complex that the uninitiated cannot make any sense of them. The stages which initiates claim to traverse in this quest are not the ones that were attained by the Prophet's Companions such as Bilāl, 'Ammār and Ṣuhaib. Nor do these stages represent anything similar to the accomplishments that stand to the credit of Abū Bakr and 'Umar.

Only those can claim some resemblance to the Islamic ideal who seek to develop piety and God-consciousness. However, piety has somehow assumed a very narrow, limited sense. Piety is supposed to consist in observing religious duties and in devoting more time and energy to the worship of Allah. This approach makes no room, however, for addressing larger issues confronting the entire society.

One's intention and role in this life

One makes preparations in accordance with one's goal. It goes without saying that every action is directed at some goal. The range of one's actions is also determined by one's overall objective. If a person has an ambitious, large-scale plan, he will naturally plan a wide range of actions as again, strategy is decided with reference to its goal. Often one does make similar preparations for different goals, but each action has an essence or spirit which is linked with the particular goal to which it is directed and, in the final stages, different paths become distinct, even though the same preparation might have been made.

Consider as an example arms manufacture. Certain similar methods of manufacture must be followed, no matter to what use the arms may be put. However, the goal in undertaking this effort invests it with a special feature in terms of the range and nature of that effort. One individual may manufacture arms with an eye to aesthetic quality, seeking to provide artistic delight to the beholder. Another may be a professional arms merchant. Yet another person may undertake such manufacture in order to use what is made in a battle. All three persons will, no doubt, draw upon similar techniques and skills for manufacturing arms. However, the different aims pursued by them distinguish them from one another. In the final stage they will stand poles apart.

The arms manufactured for artistic delight will aim only at the goal of producing exquisite pieces. These arms cannot be put to any other use than ornament. For the focus will be on their artistry, their impressive or decorous appearance, and they may be totally useless for actual fighting. Yet one working for the above goal will select only those methods that help produce decorous, fine-looking arms in order to win the admiration of those having a taste for such items. He will not have any interest in techniques that could turn those arms into lethal weapons with a wide range to attack and destroy the enemy. For these arms are not meant to inflict damage on an enemy, but designed for display, to afford onlookers with delight. Thus, someone may manufacture cannons not to win a battle but only to produce an impressive art-work. Such factories will not attract customers who need real weapons. Rather, these will attract only those with an artistic taste. They will certainly place a heavy premium on these artistic arms and use them as decoration pieces. These arms may have a very limited or nominal use as real weapons.

By contrast, a professional arms merchant will market the most deadly weapons. Far from using these arms himself, he puts them on sale. He produces for a wide range of customers – hunters, highway robbers, military adventurers and also for those striving for truth. He is not bound by any cause. Rather, others employ his arms for their respective causes. His effort is governed by the market forces in his business. To be sure he draws upon the best techniques and skills and yet he may be ignorant of the secrets of the trade. This was true of the American arms industry in the earlier part of the 20th century. It was good at manufacturing conventional weapons, but lagged behind the nations closely involved in fighting. Lloyd-George, the British Prime Minister, during the First World War, bears out the above point in remarking that American weapons, no doubt, cast a spell on others in their lustre and outward appearance. However, they were far from effective on the battlefield.

As compared to the owner merchant, one who manufactures arms for a definite military cause and who seeks to equip his army with deadly weapons, is bound to behave differently. He will, of course, follow basic principles of arms manufacturing. However, his use of these will be totally different from those of an artist or a conventional businessman. He will not attach much importance to the lustre or external beauty of his arms. Rather, all his efforts will be directed at making his arms more and more deadly and devastating. Any weapon that does not prove effective on the battleground will not have any appeal for him. If an unimpressive weapon is effective, he will instantly go for it. Impressive yet inefficient arms will not be of any interest to him. He will opt for a cannon, no matter how ugly it might be, if it can demolish forts. The same holds true for a sharp sword, though it may not outwardly have any lustre. If these weapons are also good-looking, that will be an additional feature. Nonetheless, effectiveness is the main feature of a weapon. A professional arms manufacturer does not blindly conform to conventional methods and techniques. Rather, he keeps on experimenting in his effort to produce the best. His experiments aim at originality. He may pay no attention to cosmetic arms used only for ornament. In his list of priorities, such weapons are at the top which achieve their intended result and he may therefore altogether ignore the arms produced by an artist. A professional person in this business will not sell his products to his enemy. By contrast, an artist dedicated to his art, is uninterested in the person buying his artwork. An arms dealer, however, takes great care of his customers, but is not particular about finding out their aims and objectives. An arms manufacturer given to fighting on the other hand must have in mind who his enemies and allies are. He cannot afford to provide any help or support to his enemy. He would rather destroy his arsenal with his own hands if he suspects that the enemy will

seize it, without any regard for the millions of dollars invested by
him in that arsenal.

Like arms manufacturing, self-development calls for both
intensive and extensive preparation. It involves both self-
purification and the growth of one's personality. What it signifies
is that one should free oneself of traits that are not desirable and
adorn oneself with the requisite traits. Such preparation is
synonymous with moral training. It is not an end in itself. One
should be absolutely clear in one's mind about the goal for which
this moral training is undertaken. In other words, one should
clearly decide beforehand the qualities which he should develop.
This in turn determines the rank of the person imbued with these
qualities. This helps also select suitable ways and means for
attaining self-development and the proportion in which particular
ways and means should be employed.

Man's goal and self-development

The issue of goal is central to self-development. There are various
kinds of self-development and its worth is determined with
reference to the kind pursued.

Recalling the above analogy about arms manufacture one can
easily grasp the whole issue. The crucial point is the kind of man
to be trained. Again the approach adopted may be that of the
'artist' or 'professional'. One may aim to train a group of men to
implement a scheme for material gain; alternatively, the aim may
be for the sake of attaining Allah's pleasure through the
implementation of Divine Will on earth. Many features will be
no doubt common to the training, irrespective of its goal.

Notwithstanding such common features, the men thus trained will differ from one another in line with the objective to which they are wedded, and there will be a serious divergence of opinion on the desired qualities in each case, for preferring or rejecting particular traits. What is undesirable in one instance may be highly desirable in another scheme of things. Some traits highly prized by one group will not find any mention in the worldview of others. In sum, different groups will have divergent views on the values to be developed by them and the traits which they consider as requisite and desirable. In their strategies too, they will follow different courses of action, and their priorities will accordingly vary. In sum, the man trained in one perspective will be totally different from the one who is trained in another.

Although training is a generic term, differences in its objectives and goals mean a wide variety among the persons training men for different purposes. This raises the question of how to distinguish amid the schools engaged in such training. For we need to ascertain who is after only material gains and who seeks the implementation of the divine scheme. Let us survey these different schools and compare and contrast them.

Avoiding one's obligations in this life

For an artist fundamental values are decorum, beauty, wonderful effect and their articulation. A school for self-development founded by an artist will naturally focus on these values and values antithetical to art will be barred in his school. Any deviation from artistic values will be reckoned as a major lapse. Similarly, such values as hinder the spirit of art or obstruct its blossoming or deter one from grasping the artistic meaning will be considered undesirable. The artist's main interest lies in beauty. Next in his order of preference are such values as promote artistic taste, reinforce imaginative power and develop the perception for enjoying art. To use an analogy, he may seek the manufacture of a nice radio set which looks good and is able to catch sound waves. Or he may like to have a good camera which can take high-quality pictures. An artist as such is not concerned with encounter with forces from without; he has little to do with the issues related to society, culture, politics and thought which may provoke confrontation. He is not concerned with their ideology in the world. For he does not have in mind the foundation of a structure. Rather, his interest lies only in its ornamentation, show and outward beauty. The integrity of an individual's conduct and consistency do not appeal to him in that he is after beauty alone. He is not in need of the driving force which enables one to shoulder heavy responsibilities and undertake ambitious projects. Some are interested only in quasi-spiritual powers. Accordingly they draw upon an appropriate methodology. An artist, be he a Muslim or non-Muslim, pursues the same goal. A Muslim artist may, at most, choose a strategy that is admissible in Islam selecting only the elements that suit him. He thus prepares a course of action for self-development.

Absence of the ideal

A professional artist is devoid of an ideal. In his workplace one can find models of all sorts. Dictated to by market forces he produces those items that have a good market potential. All his efforts are directed towards this goal. In this sense, he resembles the professional arms merchant who is not concerned about the identity of his customers. For the artist is not anyone's friend or enemy; at best he is neutral, non-partisan. Some may train pious people. However, the latter may serve as officials in an un-Islamic government; they may cooperate with others who are blatantly rebellious to Allah. Such training is evidently pointless.

Then there are professionals who are not very particular about traditional moral values. They may devise their own outlook on life. They train people to serve any system. They have the ability to adapt to any way of life as they pick and choose from the articles of faith, morals, spirituality and culture. Without any scruples they manage to fit in with even a wicked way of life.

Using people as cannon-fodder

There are many types of people striving for a wide range of worldly goals. Some are driven by the consideration for their own self or family, country or community. Those working for a philanthropic cause may or may not believe in faith or spirituality. What is noteworthy is that they employ several methods for training people. Common to them is their low estimation of men. For they look upon men only as agents for achieving the goal set by them. This perception permeates their training programme. In other words, far from training men they merely produce cannon-fodder. Little wonder then that their list of priorities does not have any correspondence with virtues and vices. Driven by their selfish interests they adopt a patently pragmatic and utilitarian approach. Their morality includes only those qualities which contribute to producing men of their choice. For assessing these qualities the touchstone is to examine whether they are wedded unflinchingly to higher moral values or not. They are apt to use some good qualities only for their interest. For example, they manage to infuse such discipline into men that they do not flee from a battlefield dominated by heavy, incessant bombardment. At the same time, the men trained by them cannot contain or curb their base desires even for a short time.

THE ISLAMIC CONCEPT OF SELF-DEVELOPMENT

One who trains people for the sole purpose of helping them pass the test instituted by Allah, stands out above others. For this training helps man perform his role as Allah's vicegerent on earth, to attain His pleasure by fulfilling all his obligations. In pursuit of this aim he attaches great importance to moral values. He makes a thorough and critical study of man's entire life, especially the tests and trials that he undergoes. This aspect is extensively scrutinized, with the focus on the factors which enable one to achieve success. Furthermore, he identifies divine will regarding each and every aspect of life and of the obstructions that bar man from achieving the goal. The factors from both within and without are studied and a list of priorities is drawn up. On that basis he will identify the list of desirable and undesirable qualities in one's conduct and set his priorities. This will, in turn, help him determine what force should be directed to extirpating certain evils. He will then identify a strategy for self-development. His strategy includes all such measures as remove barriers to one's inner development and which raise morale in order to challenge the external obstructions. Taken together, these will develop the traits that ensure his success and enable him to gain all that is essential for his felicity. His strategy will be permeated with the essence which is cognate with his overall objective.

The Islamic concept of self-development embraces all the above norms. Some of its terms may feature in other schools of self-development. However, this slight coincidence should not be misconstrued as total similarity. If a school of self-development prescribes certain elements not laid down by Islam, or if there is a discrepancy in the order of priorities, or if the motive is artistic or professional or otherwise this-worldly, or if there is an imbalance in the proportion suggested by the Prophet Muḥammad (peace and blessings be upon him), it is evident that the training is un-Islamic. Notwithstanding its claim to piety and purity or its commitment to some of the Islamic ideals, it cannot be taken as Islamic.

Main characteristics

Those ignorant of Islam cannot be expected to establish the Islamic order. Likewise, those not having full conviction in Islam or those who do not practise Islam in their everyday life or those not wedded to the goal of enforcing the Islamic order, cannot be entrusted with the above job. The same holds in equal measure for a group of people with the right qualities but who are disorganized, lacking in discipline, and unfamiliar with the concept of mutual consultation – their being a group cannot by itself deliver the goods.

Attachment and sincerity to Allah

Let us ascertain the main characteristics essential for achieving the objective of reform and development.

Of these the first and foremost is one's attachment and sincerity to Allah. One may embark upon anything for the sake of one's own selfish interests or those of one's family, tribe or country. An individual may commit atheism and yet achieve worldly success. No success, however, is possible in establishing the Islamic order unless one is fully committed to Allah with deep conviction and strives sincerely for this cause. For one's objective is to uphold the Word of Allah, hence one is obliged to do everything for Him. One should repose all trust in Him and look to rewards only from Him. Likewise, one should adhere strictly to His commands and fear His grip. Any dilution in one's commitment, or turning to others besides Him, will drive one away from the straight path. As a result, such efforts will not be fruitful in establishing Allah's religion.

Concern for the Hereafter

Another equally important point is concern for the Hereafter. Although this world is a believer's workplace, all his deeds are geared towards felicity in the next life. His focus is always on the consequences of his deeds in the Hereafter. Accordingly, he does all that will benefit him there and avoids all that might jeopardize his prospects there. By the same token, he should be able to bear with any loss here that may accrue rewards in the Hereafter. One's only concern should be the divine recompense and one should totally disregard loss and gain in this-worldly life. Whether one achieves success or not whether one is praised or condemned or punished or rewarded in this life, one should think only about Allah's pleasure. For, if He is pleased with the individual's efforts, and since He is All-Knowing, his reward will not be denied. Success in the Hereafter is the ultimate gain. Without this conviction one cannot proceed. If one has even some streaks of worldliness in his heart, he is bound to go astray; he will be soon demoralized on suffering some loss while working in Allah's cause. Worldliness corrupts his mind and he cannot therefore consistently pursue Allah's way.

Excellent conduct

Excellent conduct gives a person captivating influence. Those working for Allah's cause should be characterized with broad-mindedness, magnanimity, sympathy for and sincerity to mankind, large-heartedness and gentleness. Also, they should have self-respect, contentment, humility, modesty, and leniency. No one should expect any evil from them. Rather, they should do good to everyone. They should be tolerant of others and reconcile easily to giving up what is due to them. They should repulse evil with good. At least, they should not repay evil with evil. They should be appreciative of others' virtues and bear with others' lapses. Their large-heartedness should consist in their pardoning others, ignoring their wrongs and not taking revenge for personal injuries. Far from asking others to serve them, they should feel gratified in serving others and work for their interests. In performing their duty they are indifferent to public praise or condemnation and seek reward only from Allah. No one can buy or pressurize them. However, they surrender themselves readily to truth and honesty and integrity. Their excellent conduct should win over others' hearts. Equipped thus they will prove more effective than deadly weapons and more valuable than any precious asset. For such persons captivate those coming into contact with them. If a group is adorned with the above features, it assumes invincible power.

Perseverance

Another key to success is perseverance. It is a broad term with many connotations. Those working in Allah's cause should display this quality in all its varied forms.

One of its connotations is that one should not be impatient for immediate results for one's efforts, nor despair if it takes very long to get the desired results. Rather, one should consistently work for the cause, notwithstanding occasional setbacks. For social reform calls for perseverance on one's part and one lacking in this quality cannot do the job well.

Its other meaning is that one should not be capricious and fickle-minded. One should make a choice after careful reflection, then pursue that way with resolve and composure. Likewise, one should bear with all the problems in the way and put up bravely with the losses suffered by him. A persevering person remains undaunted by the onset of hardship.

Moreover, one should not betray a loose temper or be provoked easily. On the contrary, tolerance and forbearance should mark one's conduct. One who intends to carry out social reform in a society given to degeneration for long is bound to face stiff and sinister opposition to his reform programme. If he is unable to exercise self-restraint in ignoring the barrage of invectives, slander and false propaganda directed against him, he had better not take up the cause. For this way is strewn with innumerable thorns. The opponents of truth will not let him move even an inch. Therefore the reformist who takes up the issue with each and every opponent will never be in a position to embark upon his cause. In this mission only such persons are likely to gain some success whose eyes are firmly fixed on their mission and who do not waste time or energy in joining the fray with their enemies. At times, they develop differences of opinion with members of their own reform group and if they do not act with forbearance and perseverance, it will inflict irreparable damage on the cause itself.

Perseverance signifies also consistent pursuit of one's mission even in the face of temptations and fear. One should discharge one's duty in spite of the distractions and allurements suggested by Satan and the base self. This should be reflected in one's avoidance of the unlawful and adherence to the limits prescribed by Allah. One should disregard altogether the pleasures of sins and unlawful gains and be content with the losses arising out of adherence to truth. One may observe the affluence of the worldly-minded ones and yet not be drawn in the least towards them.

Rather one should willingly and confidently pursue the way which may help him win Allah's pleasure. Taken in the above sense, perseverance stands out as the key to success. Any impatience will mar the prospects of the cause of social reform and self-development.

Wisdom

Besides the above features, wisdom is another important quality on which success largely depends. All the systems of the world are being run by highly intelligent persons, drawing upon considerable material, intellectual and technological resources. It is not an easy task to displace these and establish the Islamic order in their place. This task cannot be achieved by those who have led a sheltered life. Notwithstanding their gentleness, simple-minded persons will not be able to register any success. For it calls for reflection, introspection and wisdom. Only those gifted with exceptional perspicacity about the relevant issues will be able to acquit themselves well.

Wisdom is an all-embracing term which covers all aspects of shrewd understanding. Wisdom consists in a thorough knowledge of human psychology and mutual dealings. One should not treat all persons alike, but in accordance with their different temperaments. While interacting with different individuals and groups one should act differently.

Wisdom signifies also thorough familiarity with the task and the means for performing it in the best manner. One should anticipate the problems and obstacles and overcome the opposition and resistance to the mission. This requires good understanding of the relevant issues. Above all, wisdom stands for gaining insights into faith and worldly affairs. A good jurist-consultant (*faqīh*), acquainted with *Sharī'ah* commands, may apply these to a given situation. However, training in jurisprudence is not sufficient to reform a degenerate society, to extirpate the *Jāhilī* order (un-Islamic way of life) and replace it with the Islamic one. One intending to do this should be fully conversant with the superstructure of faith as a whole, appreciate its underlying wisdom and perceive the issues related to the enforcement of *Sharī'ah* commands.

Clearing up a misconception

This account of the extensive requisites for establishing the Islamic order may make one apprehensive. For only the excellent ones can accomplish it. An ordinary person is not expected to possess all the qualities. At the very outset it should be realized that not everyone can embody all the qualities in perfect form. Nor can everyone be fully trained in the initial stages. The above account of the requisite qualities is given in order to forewarn people not to take on the task lightly, regarding it as mere community service. One should first do soul-searching in order to ascertain whether one has the potential needed for this job. If one has, one will do well to embark upon the mission. For developing and acquiring these qualities will be needed at a later stage. One may draw in this context the analogy of a seed which grows in time into a huge tree. One who has the potential is likely to develop these qualities and gradually attain excellence.

It is important to draw up a plan for reform and development. More importantly, workers who possess the requisite features are badly needed. For one has to interact with individuals and groups as part of the reform process. Therefore the workers should have the following characteristics:

- A correct understanding of faith.
- Firm conviction.
- Excellent conduct cognate with one's faith.
- A deep commitment to the realization of the goal.

A group taking up this cause should have the following qualities:

- Mutual love, respect, confidence, sincerity and self-sacrifice.
- Mutual consultation and observing its norms.
- Discipline, maintaining order and decorum, cooperation and team spirit.
- Constructive criticism in a decent manner which may stem any rot creeping into the organization. Criticism should not worsen matters.

Besides, the following features are essential to carry out the mission along the right lines and to attain real, abiding success:

- A deep commitment to Allah and working to win His pleasure.
- Constant remembrance of one's answerability in the Hereafter and disregarding all gain other than that of earning reward in the Hereafter.
- Excellent conduct.
- Perseverance.
- Wisdom

Let us now survey the main weaknesses of which the mission should be free:

Pride and arrogance

The first and foremost weakness that destroys every good deed is pride, in the form of arrogance, self-exaltation and boastfulness. Satan incites one to indulge in these weaknesses, which are incompatible with the mission for reform and self-development. All greatness belongs to Allah alone. One's claim to exaltation is sheer falsehood. Whoever suffers from it is denied any divine help and support. For Allah abhors this trait most. Those afflicted with it cannot recover. Nor can they ever be guided to the straight way. They keep on committing one mistake after another, culminating in their total loss and destruction. The more they behave arrogantly towards others, the more revulsion they evoke. They stand so much discredited that they do not enjoy any moral authority over others.

This affliction strikes those devoted to the cause of truth in a variety of ways. As they improve somewhat morally and spiritually in comparison to other members of the degenerate society and their contribution is publicly acclaimed, Satan incites them to indulge in pride and arrogance. Prompted thus by Satan they talk very highly of themselves. The mission on which they had embarked in all piety tends to get adulterated. Another possible scenario is that those engaged in their own self-development and in reforming others, no doubt, stand out above others in their morals. They have to their credit some good deeds. They naturally become conscious of these points. However, their momentary lapse and Satan's incitement misdirect them to the path of arrogance and self-exaltation.

When their opponents find fault with them, in their self-defence they recount their achievements. If care is not exercised, this can quickly degenerate into pride and arrogance. Every individual and organization should avoid it. Those taking up this mission should realize all along that they are the servants of Allah and that greatness befits Allah alone. Man is His slave, hence he should act humbly. Only by Allah's grace is one able to accomplish anything. On one's own one cannot achieve anything. Far from becoming proud, one should be all the more grateful to Him. Whatever one has should be dedicated to the cause of Allah which will help him earn more reward. Indulgence in pride is tantamount to committing evil and opting for the path of error.

Apart from an acute sense of being human, self-examination can also deter one from indulging in pride. One should regularly do soul-searching, with a view to identifying shortcomings and lapses. Whoever does this regularly cannot fall prey to self-exaltation, as he is so preoccupied with seeking Allah's pardon for his lapses that he cannot afford to grow proud.

The observation of role models that make one sharply aware of one's shortcomings can also deter pride. Morals and spirituality are marked by lofty heights and abysmal depths. Even a die-hard culprit may consider himself better than some. This, however, makes him more complacent. Furthermore, Satan suggests to him that he can go down further in the pursuit of his misdeeds. Those bent on self-destruction follow this line of thinking. However, genuine seekers of truth and self-development always focus their attention on perfect role models. Doing so torments them in that they come to see their own flaws and imperfections and are then driven to see new heights of piety and excellence.

A group working for the cause of truth should always be on the alert. It should promptly take note of any tendency to pride and self-exaltation. This should be nonetheless checked in a way that does not breed false modesty and affectation. For this is the worst form of pride.

Showing off and seeking popularity

If individuals or groups undertake their mission only for the sake of fame or public applause, it strikes at the roots of the mission itself. It is something antithetical to faith and appropriately branded an implicit form of polytheism. One's belief in Allah and the Hereafter demands that one perform deeds only for the sake of gaining Allah's pleasure. One should expect all reward only from Him and set one's eyes on the recompense in the Hereafter. However, a hypocrite is only after public acclaim and demands his reward from fellow human beings. His main interest lies in amassing fame, popularity, power, authority and glory. To put it otherwise, he takes creatures as partners with Allah. In this case all his efforts, however substantial they might be, are not directed exclusively to Allah. He will not, therefore, be reckoned as pious by Allah.

An impious motive has an adverse effect on one's efforts for the cause. In fact, one cannot do any real good if one is prompted by selfish motives. Such an individual is given totally to self-publicity, attaching importance only to what serves that end. He disregards all those deeds performed quietly only for pleasing Allah. His sphere of action thus narrows down to those actions that add to his fame. His interest in the mission wanes, though he may have been sincere in the initial stage. Attachment to publicity kills his sincerity and he is no longer able to discharge his duties. His perception changes altogether as he sees everything from the prism of seeking and gaining publicity and fame. Accordingly he pays more attention to actions that are approved by the public but detests actions that may decrease his popularity, even though these may be important tasks for the cause of truth.

Those leading a secluded life in a monastic lodge are largely immune from the temptation of fame. However, those who appear on the public scene with the avowed mission of reform are always vulnerable to it. They can become infected by it at any time. They have to do many things to draw public attention. The nature of their work demands that they bring out and circulate their progress reports. Some of the measures introduced by them win public approval and they are publicly praised for their accomplishments. Likewise, they face opposition to their mission and in self-defence they may have to highlight, however unwillingly, their positive contribution. Given this, it is really hard for them to avoid the temptations of publicity and fame. They have to take extra care that earning fame should not become their main objective. Surrounded by hypocrites they should shun hypocrisy. Obviously it calls for painstaking efforts, self-restraint and hard work. For any slight negligence may open a way to hypocrisy in their conduct.

Both individual and collective efforts should be made to check it. As to the former, it consists in performing certain deeds secretly, and regular self-criticism. The individual should ascertain for himself whether he is more keenly interested in public or private virtues. On sensing a greater interest in deeds performed for public consumption, he should immediately curb any hypocrisy on his part. Seeking refuge with Allah, he should strive to check his base self and amend his approach.

A group or organization working for this cause should ensure that no hypocrisy creeps into its activism. It should notify its achievements in a modest way. If it is feared that this may lead to ostentation, this should be immediately checked. No measure should be adopted merely to be populist; nor should any measure be avoided merely because it may be disliked by the public. The organization should develop and promote a milieu in which its activists are keen to discharge their duties, without regard for public praise or criticism. If some members of the group betray an inclination to name and fame, remedial steps should be taken.

Bad intention

Any impiety in one's intention cannot obviously result in good. With a pure intention alone can one accomplish any good. It goes without saying that the objective is to promote good and thus gain Allah's pleasure. It should not be adulterated with any personal or group motive. Nor should one expect any material gain as this will deprive one of Allah's reward. No one can achieve much even in this world if his loyalty is divided. Such division affects the person's character, and a weakened, troubled character cannot attain success in a mission aimed at extirpating evil and establishing good.

For a mission on a limited scale it is not hard to preserve one's integrity and purity of intention. Attachment to Allah and sincerity of purpose may suffice. However, those striving for the reform of the entire way of life and reconstructing it along Islamic lines cannot rest content with only propagating their views or exhorting others or seeking moral uplift. They have to make efforts, directly and indirectly, to reorient the political order. This inevitably entails that they either assume political power themselves or that such power be in the hands of a group supported by them. In either case the concept of power is intertwined with the political order. Given this, the reformers cannot avoid politics. They cannot escape the label of those seeking power. The situation calls for self-restraint and self-discipline. One should first grasp the essential difference between seeking power for themselves or for a cause. Since a total change is sought, the political order cannot be disregarded. It is imperative that political authority should be transferred to them or to a group supported by them. Yet there is a world of difference between seeking power for selfish motives and for and on behalf of principles and ideals. The two differ greatly in essence. The former admits impurity of purpose while the latter represents an ideal. One should devote oneself heart and soul to the latter. For this, there is the role model of the Prophet (peace and blessings be upon him) and the Companions. They sought to transform the whole way of life. To do so they had to assume political power. In its absence they could not uphold faith in its entirety. As a result of their sustained struggle they did acquire political authority. However, they cannot be suspected of having undertaken this mission for political power. There have been, on the other hand, innumerable instances of the seekers of power for selfish ends. The two stand poles apart in their intention, which is borne out also by their conduct and its consequences.

Those wedded to the ideal of the total domination of Islam in all walks of life should realize the above difference and adhere to the straight way. They should never fall into the trap of seeking power for selfish ends. Any weakness on this count breeds many other shortcomings. Imbalance is a serious cause of weakness. Initially one may not regard it as a serious flaw. However, it turns out to be a major flaw with devastating effects. Want of moderation in thought and deeds leads one astray. Moreover, it always results in failure which strikes a deadly blow to an organization championing the cause of collective welfare and reconstruction.

Imbalance and extremism

Imbalance is betrayed by a one-sided approach to things. Overcome by emotions one looks at things from a particular angle while neglecting other relevant aspects. One pursues a particular course of action and pays no attention to other points. This results in an imbalance in thinking. One reckons only one point as important and underrates other equally significant points. Likewise, one identifies a certain evil as the root cause at the expense of ignoring other major evils. On the issue of rules and principles, one fails to exhibit any flexibility. Conversely, one too keen to get things done may show an utter disdain for norms and employ all ways and means to attain 'success', without any scruples about norms and rules.

This tendency gives way ultimately to extremism. For one who insists on his stance, takes a harsh stand against any dissident voice. He fails to consider others' viewpoint and makes no effort to weigh things justly. Rather, he ascribes the worst motives to divergent views. This makes him as quite unbearable to others. If this tendency is not checked in time, it culminates in suspecting others' integrity, bad temper and use of harsh language, which inflicts a deadly blow upon solidarity.

If an individual behaves thus, he will be cut off from the organization and sever his relations with the group which he had joined to accomplish a noble objective. However, if this trend gains currency among members of a group, it gives birth to an extremist group. Others set up, in reaction, another group to oppose it. Mutual differences culminate in rift and schism and as a result, the cause suffers most.

There are many tasks which can be performed only by a group, not by individuals. One has to work in close association with and persuade others. It does not put an end to the differences in temperaments, attitudes, talents and individual traits. Notwithstanding these variations, mutual relations are essential and unavoidable. This calls for understanding and adjustment. This can be displayed by those gifted with a balanced, moderate personality. If immoderate persons join a group, they cannot remain united to it or each other for long. Their organization is bound to disintegrate. It will eventually result in divisions and subdivisions.

Those working for the cause of Islam and committed to the ideal of establishing an Islamic order should do soul-searching and avoid imbalance in any form. The organization should ensure that this weakness does not afflict its ranks. On this count they should follow the guidance imparted by the Qur'ān and the *Ḥadīth*. Both of these primary Islamic sources forbid extremism in any form. The Qur'ān holds the People of the Book guilty of committing excesses in faith (al-Nisā' 4:171). The Prophet (peace and blessings be upon him) warned his Companions thus: 'Beware! Do not indulge in extremism. For earlier communities were destroyed on account of their extremism.' (Aḥmad) According to Ibn Mas'ūd, in one of his sermons the Prophet (peace and blessings be upon him) reiterated the following point thrice: 'They were destroyed who indulged in extremism, exaggeration and excesses.' (Muslim) His directive was: 'Make allowance. Do not put people to inconvenience. Give glad tidings. Do not provoke hostility and revulsion.' (Bukhārī and Muslim) 'Allah is lenient. He prefers leniency on every count.' (Bukhārī and Muslim) 'One who is not lenient is denied all good.' (Muslim)

Keeping in mind that guidance, if those working for the cause of Islam avoid selecting only that from the Qur'ān and the *Sunnah* what suits them, they will naturally develop the balance and moderation to shape life in accordance with the Qur'ānic model.

Meanness

Meanness is yet another major weakness. The Qur'ān condemns it and classes those as the successful ones who shun it. For meanness runs counter to piety and doing good. One afflicted with it makes no allowance for others, nor grants space to them. While he seeks every favour and relaxation for himself, he does not grant any indulgence or favour to others. For him his own virtues are excellent while the same in others are dismissed by him as a matter of chance. He justifies all his lapses while he is not ready to forgive others. He makes much of the hardships faced by himself whereas he regards the difficulties encountered by others as a mere pretext. He is not prepared to give any allowance to others for even the same mistakes which he himself commits. Without any concern for others he demands of others hard work which he himself does not perform. Likewise, he imposes his views upon others and does not care at all for others' opinions. This aggravates further into finding fault with everyone. While he takes others to task for their minor lapses, he resents any accountability for his own actions. This obviously results in intolerance. He becomes a trial to those who come into contact with him.

Any organization suffering from this malaise is only too vulnerable. The requirement for collective work calls for mutual love and cooperation. Meanness puts an end to solidarity. Instead, it sours mutual relations and provokes hatred and hostility. Those suffering from it are not fit to lead a normal social life. It is antithetical to the qualities needed to lead a life in accordance with Islam. For Islam promotes tolerance, generosity, forgiveness and large-heartedness. Only those endowed with forbearance and perseverance are suited for carrying out its mission. They are strict towards themselves and lenient to others. They reckon good qualities in others while they are acutely conscious of their own lapses. Far from hurting others they withstand all hardships and rescue others. A group made up of such noble souls will demonstrate unity and attract all members of the society. By contrast, a motley gang of mean and narrow-minded people is bound to disintegrate soon and arouse sheer revulsion in others.

CHAPTER 2

Self-development and its Role in Life

Muḥammad Fārūq Khān

THE ROLE OF FAITH IN LIFE

Self-development is a scientific as well as religious term. To grasp its nature and its importance in faith we should first recall the role of faith in life. Those who have reflected deeply on religion recognize that Allah demands of man only those obligations cognate with his essential nature. Likewise, Allah takes man to task for only those deeds that man himself regards as abhorrent. The Qur'ān states: 'So set your face towards the True Faith uprightly. And follow the constitution of Allah according to which He has constituted mankind and let there be no alteration in Allah's creation. That is the right religion.' (al-Rūm 30:30) That every new-born child has a natural disposition is stated in *ḥadīth*.

Man draws naturally towards Allah, like iron is attracted towards a magnet or as a flame rises upward. All those things that prompt man to draw closer towards Allah are therefore regarded as beneficial in that these bring immense blessings and ultimate felicity. In contrast, all that distracts man from Allah is regarded in *Sharī'ah* as sinful, since it causes corruption. One committing a sin wrongs himself.

If man is purged of his negative traits such as narrow-mindedness, parochialism, selfish desires and wickedness, his essentially good nature blossoms in full. He is characterized by such positive traits as large-heartedness, forbearance, insight, tolerance and concern for others. In this state man can draw heavily upon his Lord. This marks his perfection. Faith stands for perfecting man. Society is needed to enable man to attain his perfection. The construction of a society is not however, a goal in itself. The *Sharī'ah* focuses on individuals. On the Day of Judgement everyone will have to render his account in his individual capacity. It is no doubt true that the way prescribed by the Qur'ān for perfection involves society in that man cannot attain it on his own. Yet the goal is individual growth and perfection. Moreover, Islam's vision of society provides room for every individual to attain his perfection, indeed, society contributes to his reaching that goal. This is a distinctive feature of the Islamic social system.

Allah's attributes are recurrently mentioned in the Qur'ān, directing man to gain the understanding of divine attributes and appreciate the essence and spirit of divine commands. According to the Qur'ān, 'Allah loves those who do good.' (Āl 'Imrān 3:148) Contained in the above verse is the exhortation to do good to others oneself and like Allah, to love those persons who do good. The Qur'ān further declares: 'And be you generous as Allah has been generous to you, and seek not corruption in the land. Allah approves not corrupters.' (al-Qaṣaṣ 28:77) If one abandons the way of doing good it entails corruption on earth, and Allah abhors those responsible for causing disorder. At another place the Qur'ān instructs: 'Do justice. Verily Allah loves those who do justice.' (al-Ḥujurāt 49:9) Allah asks man to develop in himself a reflection of divine attributes, no matter however faint the reflection might be. By this grace alone man is endowed with sense perception: in that Allah is All-Hearing and All-Seeing, man is blessed by Him with the faculties of hearing and sight. Similarly, as He accomplishes whatever He wills, He has conferred upon some a measure of freedom of choice and volition. By the same token, He wills that man adorn himself with excellent morals and manners. The point is borne out by the *ḥadīth*: 'Allah is gentle; He loves gentleness.' (Muslim) It is recorded in another *ḥadīth*: The Prophet (peace and blessings be upon him) stated: 'Allah is the most generous. Of all men I am the most generous one. Next to me are those who gain knowledge and impart it. Such will appear as leaders on the Day of Judgement, as a community unto themselves.' (Bayhaqī)

One of the divine attributes is that Allah is independent of everyone. It therefore befits man to grow independent of everyone while reposing all trust in Allah alone. One should turn to Allah for all his needs and depend wholly upon Him. Of course, man cannot become independent of Allah. For his very existence and survival he depends on Allah. Likewise, he cannot turn away from Him for meeting his needs. Man is the servant of Allah alone. It does not behove him to serve anyone besides Him. The Qur'ān proclaims: 'Ours is the dye of Allah and who is better at dyeing than Allah? And we are His worshippers.' (al-Baqarah 2:138) Since Allah is Most Holy, man is obliged to follow the way of purity. By the same token, as He is Most Merciful, we should be merciful towards others. Without this we cannot serve Him adequately.

The true meaning of self-development

The foregoing highlights the important role of faith in man's life. For faith directs man to achieve perfection. Self-development consists in attaining this perfection. Man is a moral being, and accordingly, the *Sharī'ah* is concerned, in the main, with morals. Self-development enables man to excel in morals. The essence of faith and *Sharī'ah* resides in cleansing and perfecting man's self. The Qur'ān makes the point in this way: '[Abraham petitioned:] Our Lord! Raise up for them a Messenger from among them who will recite to them Your Revelation and will teach the Book and wisdom, and will cleanse them.' (al-Baqarah 2:129)

A Messenger is charged with the responsibility of reciting the Word of God to people, of instructing them in *Sharī'ah* and wisdom and this, in turn, cleanses them. In some other Qur'ānic passages cleansing is mentioned first, followed by the reference to teaching the Book and wisdom. (For example, verses 151 of al-Baqarah, 164 of Āl 'Imrān and 2 of al-Jumu'ah.) As the objective, self-development is mentioned first, while instruction (in wisdom and knowledge) is the means to that end. That self-development is the ultimate objective of faith is illustrated by the following Qur'ānic verse: 'Surely he succeeds who has cleansed it [his soul], and he fails who has buried it.' (al-Shams 91:9-10) The verse states unequivocally that self-development lies at the heart of faith, and it brings out the meaning and purport of self-development. Any neglect in cleansing the soul results in its being destroyed and 'buried'. The same expression, *tadsiyyah*, is used elsewhere in the Qur'ān when the Arab polytheists learned of the birth of a baby daughter, their faces darkened and they felt deeply hurt and humiliated. They instinctively thought of burying her alive in order to avoid disgrace: 'Shall he keep it with ignominy or bury it in the dust?' (al-Naḥl 16:59)

In contrast *tazkiyah* signifies causing something to grow towards its perfection and full development. Self-development aims at realizing one's potentials without any hindrance. There is nothing essentially abominable in human nature which must then be blunted or suppressed. Islam does not prescribe monasticism. It is a distinctive feature of Islam that it does not stigmatize any bounty granted by Allah. Included in this are food items, sexual desire or one's pursuit of power or leadership. Islam nonetheless asks man to act within the prescribed limits. It views natural urges in a positive light and accords them their rightful place.

Had Islam been wedded to the goal of monasticism, it would not have suggested self-development as a desirable goal. For, by its very definition it represents the growth and development of the soul. Some narrowly misconstrue it in the sense of purification. Of course, one should be free from all impurities. Yet it is a positive, comprehensive term. The Qur'ān observes: 'Assuredly We have created man in the best mould. Thereafter We revert him to the lowest of the low, save those who believe and work righteous deeds. Theirs shall be reward unending.' (al-Tīn 95:4-6) The above passage underscores the following truths:

i.   Allah has created man both inwardly and outwardly in the best mould. Allah has placed immense good in man;

what is needed is to develop his innate positive traits. However, *Jāhilīyah* (ignorance) and degenerate society cloud man's essential goodness. Man should regain his natural state, overcoming all the barriers to it.

ii. Man's creation in the best mould signifies his elevated status. Any deviation from the natural way amounts to self-abasement. This point is eloquently made in the above Qur'ānic passage that those who debase themselves are reverted to the lowest of the low.

iii. It goes without saying that those who appreciate their elevated status are most likely to avoid a fall. They are aware of their role and responsibilities. They do not suffer from any confusion and hence consistently follow the way which befits their exalted position.

iv. Since these conscientious persons do not act against self-reform, and do not weaken their essential goodness by tainting their self, they do not encounter any loss or despair.

v. Their unending reward points to the working of a consistent moral order in the universe. Faith does not impose any unnatural restriction. On the contrary, it represents the completion of divine bounty, which is immensely beneficial for man. In response to this great divine favour man can only express his deep sense of gratitude to Him, as is specified in the Qur'ān: 'Allah does not mean to lay upon you a hardship, but means to purify you and to complete His favour upon you that perhaps you may return thanks.' (al-Mā'idah 5:6)

As already stated self-development is the ultimate goal set by faith, a point substantiated by verse 9 of *al-Shams*. Other verses of a similar import are cited below: 'The Day wherein neither riches nor sons will be of any avail. Unless it be he who shall bring to Allah a whole heart.' (al-Shu'arā' 26:88-89) In other words, in the sight of Allah only they are successful who preserve the natural goodness that Allah has infused into them. Those who follow the natural way are expected to maintain the wholeness of the heart. Elsewhere it is recorded in the Qur'ān: 'And to the pious Paradise will be brought near, not far off. This is what you were promised, for every oft-returning heedful one, who fears the Compassionate in the unseen and comes to Him with a penitent heart.' (Qāf 50:31-33) The truly successful ones are those who turn penitently to Allah. They do not taint their essential self. Rather, they guard dutifully what is entrusted to them.

Another relevant Qur'ānic passage is as follows: 'And he who comes to Him as a believer, and has done righteous deeds, then for them are high ranks. Gardens everlasting with running streams, abiding therein; that is the reward for him who has purified himself.' (Ṭā Hā 20:75-76) Self-development accrues the reward of high rank and success in the Hereafter. Moreover, self-development is inconceivable without faith and good deeds to one's credit. In the Qur'ānic parlance, a person who has purified himself is the one who possesses faith and regularly does good deeds. Here is another Qur'ānic passage: 'Surely those who sell Allah's covenant and their oaths at a small price, no portion is theirs in the Hereafter. Nor shall Allah speak to them nor look at them on the Day of Judgement. Nor shall He purify them, and theirs shall be a painful torment.' (Āl 'Imrān 3:77)

One learns from that verse that man's true and abiding success consists in securing self-development. Allah describes such persons as successful and will bestow upon them more bounties out of

His grace. They will enjoy felicity in the Hereafter. Allah will speak to them and shower His mercy upon them. Those who have attained self-development are neither characterless nor reckless in their commitments.

Effects of self-development

Self-development brings about astonishing results. The Qur'ān teaches: 'He indeed has attained bliss who has cleansed himself, and who remembers the names of his Lord, and then prays. Nay! (but) you prefer the life of this world, whereas the Hereafter is far better and more lasting. This is in the Books of Abraham and Moses.' (al-A'lā 87:14-19). This passage contains a succinct account of the impact of self-development on man. Everyone is obliged to strive for it. The quest for it is helped and supported by Allah. For it is He Who blesses man with it, as is adumbrated in the Qur'ān: 'Have you not observed those who hold themselves to be pure? Nay, it is Allah Who purifies whom He pleases. But never will they fail to receive justice in the least little thing.' (al-Nisā' 4:49) Again: 'And had there not been Allah's grace upon you and His mercy, not one of you could ever have been cleansed, but Allah cleanses whom He will, and Allah is All-Hearing, All-Knowing.' (al-Nūr 24:21) Remembering the names of the Lord, seeking to understand the meaning of His attributes, and offering prayers – these are some of the results of self-development, which serve also as the means to it. No one can approach to any perfection by disregarding Allah. It is necessary that one should be cognizant of His being and attributes. In fact one should be fired by the quest to draw closer to Allah. Prayer is an outward manifestation of the urge to gain nearness to Allah.

This urge is not merely psychological. It ennobles man in carrying him away from the mortal to the immortal and elevates him from the lower to the higher rank. In return for this effort on man's part, Allah blesses him with eternal life and an abode representing the ever-lasting Paradise. He will be further blessed in Paradise with the glimpse of the divine. On the Day of Judgement therefore, some faces will be radiant, turning fully to Allah. (al-Qiyāmah 75:22-23) At the other end of the scale, there will be some to whom these rewards will be denied altogether: 'By no means! On that Day they will be shut out from their Lord. Then they will be roasted in the scorching hell.' (al-Muṭaffifīn 83:15-16)

Self-development leads to the eternal and blissful life in the Hereafter while its neglect incurs loss, punishment and destruction. The Qur'ān issues a dire warning to unbelievers, not to be swayed by falsehood. They are asked to focus on self-development. Since perfection is in their own interest, they should devote themselves to it. When they neglect prayer, their lives become devoid of serious purpose or depth. They are ignorant of the next life that is ever-lasting, unable to appreciate the abiding happiness therein. Evidently this is a great loss. They ought to have realized the importance of life in the next world. The benefits contingent upon self-development figure in both the Qur'ān and earlier Scriptures. Throughout time there has been a single route to success and felicity, the one to which Messengers invited their respective communities.

Good deeds and self-development

As already indicated, there are certain ways and means of attaining self-development. One who cleanses his self of worldliness, greed and selfishness is not troubled at all by the prospect of spending in Allah's way. Rather, he experiences sheer delight and contentment in giving charity and paying *zakāh*. Charity reinforces the spirit and its purity. The Qur'ān speaks thus of those Muslims who have both good and evil deeds to their credit and who confess their wrongdoings: 'Take alms from their riches; thereby you will cleanse them and purify them, and pray for them. Your prayer is a solace for them.' (al-Tawbah 9:103) Alms-giving contributes to self-development. It helps one overcome worldliness and greed. The Prophet's prayer blessed these Muslims with peace of mind and tranquillity. Like charity, other good deeds also, help achieve self-development.

One who is committed to self-development, he may be taken as a trustworthy person who does not fail in obeying divine commands. He discharges efficiently the duty assigned to him. Furthermore, he grows as a God-fearing person, who is continuously aware of divine glory and might. He internalizes morals derived from a sound understanding of divine attributes. As a devout servant of the Lord of all the worlds he cannot be the cause of any mischief nor succumbs to the divisiveness rooted in ethnic, national or cultural prejudice. He is not self-centred. On the contrary, his vision is universal and he works for the benefit of the whole of mankind. He seeks the same success for others that he desires for himself. The Prophet (peace and blessings be upon him) observed: 'You will be a Muslim, if you prefer for others what you like for yourself.'

Self-development does not leave any room for narrowness or parochialism in that one does not and cannot opt for self-interest in preference to truth. He does not follow the criteria of honour and disgrace professed and practised by misguided communities. He recognizes that injustice is ruinous for mankind, for in the midst of widespread injustice man cannot discharge his obligations towards the One True God. He recognizes that he will face obstructions at every step erected by the forces of falsehood. For example, if he resolves to extirpate obscenity and nudity, he will be opposed tooth and nail by those in power, who would rather promote obscenity. Likewise, his decision to put an end to the evils of usury and wine will be negated by an un-Islamic state that grants free licence for selling and buying wine. A person adorned with self-development works ceaselessly for improvements in public morality and for preaching godliness. In contrast, those in power resort to all means to defend their privileged position, even at the expense of sacrificing morals, justice and equality. History bears abundant witness to this bitter reality.

On the contrary, when the pious ones assume power and authority, they act in an altogether different fashion, as the Qur'ān attests: 'Those who, if We establish them in the land, will establish prayer and pay *zakāh* and command what is reputable and restrain what is disreputable; and unto Allah is the end of all affairs.' (al-Ḥajj 22:41) In other words, no flaw mars their conduct. For they fulfill the obligations due to Allah and to fellow human beings. Moreover, they promote and enjoin good and curb and forbid evil. They provide the best arrangements for the moral training of the public. While performing these duties they are ever conscious of the Hereafter. They entrust all affairs to Allah. Given this, the votaries of truth are not shaken by temporary set-backs and suffering. They prefer death to compromise with falsehood. In all circumstances they are loyal to the truth and abhor collusion with wrongdoers. Their supplication, as recorded in the Qur'ān, is reflective of their mind-set: 'O Allah, Sovereign of the Dominion! You give dominion to whom You will. You exalt whom You will and You abase whom You will. And in Your hand is good; surely You are Powerful over everything.' (Āl 'Imrān 3:26) This explains the Qur'ānic view of subjugation. It is a disgrace for the champions of truth to lead a life of enslavement. On assuming power they do not enslave anyone. Far from acting on their whims or base desires, they always abide by divine commands. The Islamic concept of self-development is very broad. It is not restricted to one's inner self or spiritual aspect. Rather, it embraces man's entire thought, record of deeds and both his personal and social life.

Only they manage to attain self-development who are conscientious, are very particular about the limits prescribed by Allah and realize the onerous responsibility of leading mankind which is assigned to the Muslim community. This is what constitutes piety. Without piety there cannot be any self-development. The Qur'ān employs the above two terms as synonyms: 'Do not ascribe purity to yourselves. He is the best Knower of him who fears Him.' (al-Najm 53:32)

Call for self-development

The Qur'ānic call is directed at men urging them to seek self-development. Illustrative of it is the following passage: 'Has there come to you the story of Moses? Recall when your Lord called to him in the holy valley of Ṭuwā: "Go you to Pharaoh; verily he has vexed exorbitant." Then say: "Would you be purified? I shall guide you to your Lord, so that you shall fear."' (al-Nāziʿāt 79:15-19) The Prophet Moses's call to Pharaoh was designed to salvage him from his abased state. Man cannot proceed in the right direction, unless he possesses and acts on divine guidance. Arrogance, rebellion and egotism are traits that drive one away from Allah. Fear of Allah is indicative of one's nearness to Him, as the realization of divine might and glory humbles man and mellows his heart. It is in this state that he perceives subtle truths. Without it, he cannot and does not possess the spirit which is demanded by true faith, nor is he blessed with the necessary wisdom. Self-development brings immense reward. It can be gained by only those who fear Allah and regularly establish prayer: 'You can warn only those who fear their Lord, unseen, and establish prayer. And whosoever becomes cleansed, becomes cleansed only for himself and to Allah is the return.' (Fāṭir 35:18) Obviously everyone has to return to Allah. However, those will enjoy honour who manage to achieve self-development and thus adorn themselves. Those neglectful of it will be utter losers, unable to compensate their loss in any way in the Hereafter.

Ways and means for self-development

Let us identify the ways and means for self-development, which is urged by the Qur'ān and for the preaching of which the Prophet Muḥammad (peace and blessings be upon him) was sent down. The following Qur'ānic passage states in no uncertain terms that the Prophet (peace and blessings be upon him) was assigned the task of promoting self-development: 'Our Lord! Raise up for them a Messenger from among them, who will recite to them Your revelation and will teach them the Book and wisdom and purify them. Surely You alone are the Mighty, Wise.' (al-Baqarah 2:129) The essence of *Sharīʿah* consists in self-development. The verse just cited identifies ways and means to attain it. A Messenger recites to his community divine revelation, instructs them in the Book and wisdom and thus enables them to achieve self-development. This goal is not attainable without passing through this process. Even a Messenger cannot instantly bless someone with it, investing him with the character that is acceptable to Allah. Rather, his strategy rests on the following components: (i) recitation of Qur'ānic verses, (ii) teaching the Book and (iii) instructing in wisdom. These components touch on every department of human life and constitute the essentials of faith. One cannot achieve self-development whilst disregarding any of these components. Let us discuss each of these components separately.

i. *Reciting Qur'ānic verses*

It is essential for self-development that one should recite or listen to Qur'ānic verses. The Word of God captivates the mind and heart at the same time. Many were won over to Islam by the spell cast by the Qur'ānic recitation. Its melody and rhythm so enthralled that they eventually managed to steer themselves away from the path of error. Besides embodying the best message, the Qur'ān caters also for man's tastes and natural urges. There is simply no alternative to recitation of the Qur'ān; it serves, in a sense, as a 'dialogue' with Allah, with the believer hearing Allah address him directly. According to the Qur'ān, believers grow in faith on listening to its verses (al-Anfāl 8:2). At another place, the following observation is recorded: 'When the verses of the Most Compassionate One are recited to them, they fall down in prostration, crying.' (Maryam 19:58) One thus learns that the Qur'ān's recitation is instrumental in building and strengthening man's personality and in awakening man's spirit and inner being. Without it one cannot develop a sound moral sense.

ii. *Instructing in the Book*

The Book signifies divine commands and directives communicated to man through the agency of the Messenger. One who is ignorant of these cannot appreciate the true meaning and dimension of self-development. Nor will he have any idea about the ideal society. The Book informs one of the divine attributes of mercy and justice. By acting on divine command man can establish peace, security and justice in the land. In the absence of this knowledge one cannot embark upon the goal of removing corruption and injustice. One will have no charter to offer to mankind.

Moreover, on studying the Book one realizes that the code of conduct and commands prescribed by Allah are not for study alone. These commands are essential for mankind. The individual cannot enact them on his own, therefore he is obliged to prepare an atmosphere conducive to their implementation. To be more precise, we should adopt the same strategy that was employed by the Prophet Muḥammad (peace and blessings be upon him) for their implementation.

iii. *Imparting wisdom*

Wisdom is of crucial importance to self-development. As to its nature, wisdom is enlightenment and insight. It may be manifested in a variety of forms. It characterizes the minds and hearts, and the conduct, of the devout. It is reflected in the virtues of purity, gratitude, gratefulness, generosity and excellent character. Wisdom, in sum, is the fountainhead of all that is good. Little wonder then that the Qur'ān proclaims that one endowed with wisdom is blessed with immense good (al-Baqarah 2:269). One blessed with it leads life as a grateful servant of Allah. He can never grow disobedient or ungrateful to Him. Illustrative of it is the Qur'ānic role model of Luqmān, who, endowed with wisdom, was ever full of gratitude to Allah. Wisdom thus consists in turning gratefully to Allah. Other virtues such as truthfulness, generosity and piety are embedded in wisdom. Those joining the company of a wise person benefit greatly. This explains why the Prophet's Companions stand out above others in their wisdom. After reciting the Qur'ān, gaining understanding of divine commands and developing insights and wisdom one will naturally strive to perfect the self. Nothing can distract him, mislead him into error and fallacy. The ways and means prescribed by the Qur'ān are sufficient for guidance on this path – one need not draw on any other source. Nor is there any more exalted station than occupying the enviable position of having attained self-development. The above components provide man with everything that he needs. The Qur'ānic guidance should become an inseparable part of one's being. For it transforms one altogether. One does not lose anything in the process; rather, one may gain an indescribable spiritual ecstasy. In the effort for self-development one appreciates better the import of the following perceptive observation: 'Man is rich according to what he is, not according to what he has.' Another apt remark in this context is: 'Not to do but to be is the mark of a real practitioner.' A person may do good, but it does not prove that he is a pious person. A wicked individual may also do a good deed – to gain reputation or for ostentation. In contrast, a pious person embodies the virtues in his being and his actions. Fear of Allah helps one grow into such an embodiment of the virtues.

MORAL VALUES

In essence morals are something imperceptible, but they are reflected in one's conduct. In making moral choices one must be free to exercise judgement, to accept or decline an offer or opportunity. One must enjoy the freedom to choose a way of life and, on this basis, one is held responsible for his actions since one acts from choice not compulsion. In the absence of a free exercise of volition, the moral issue does not arise. Plants, animals and inanimate objects are not governed by morals and owe no responsibility. Plants and inanimate objects are insentient; animals are guided only by their instincts and accordingly follow a set path that does not admit any deviancy. Without morals, character is not subject to 'development' – development or degradation are alike meaningless in this case.

Of all the creatures in the universe man alone is linked with morals and accordingly his self may improve or degenerate.

When opting for a path man takes into account its good and evil, profit and harm, peace and insecurity, success and loss. Those with myopic vision are concerned only with short-term gains, blind to the long-term effects of their actions. It is important to bear in mind that everyone holds a particular worldview, including the concept and purpose of life. It is a separate issue that the worldview may be fallacious – one may have a patently materialistic or overtly spiritual worldview – but it nonetheless determines one's concept of good and evil, loss and gain. A materialistic person may have an entirely different perception of things from that of a spiritually-oriented person.

A fallacious concept of the purpose of life and of man's role and status in this world, will adversely affect one's moral vision. It will entail disorder on a global scale. Man innately discerns between good and evil. The German philosopher, Kant, while maintaining that reason cannot fathom everything was compelled to acknowledge the existence of a sense of morality. Man's freedom is, no doubt, precious in that it ensures his development and creativity. However, an abuse of freedom results only in his destruction.

We are not concerned in this work to draw any comparison between Islam and other faiths with regard to their stance on morals. Nor do we intend to survey critically the views of leading thinkers and philosophers on the subject. We will not deal either with the Western approach to morals. Rather, our focus will be on the Islamic position.

The Islamic worldview

Islam clearly states that the universe is Allah's creation and that He has made it subservient to mankind. Since the universe and mankind are Allah's creation, the whole scheme of things represents the grand divine plan. All that exists reflects His glory and perfection. Allah's being is free from any imperfection and is characterized by all that is good. He is not subject to decline. He is the Ever-Living, Self-Subsisting God, the source of all knowledge, virtue and beauty. All affairs are referred to Him for His final judgement. He is the fountainhead of generosity, mercy, compassion and love. He has invested everything with a sense of purpose, beauty and attraction. Little wonder then that all beings glorify Him. He has blessed man with the best feelings, emotions, urges and creative power which accounts for variety. He does not approve inaction, despair and depression, whereas freedom, joy, beauty and attractiveness are encouraged by Him.

In the Islamic scheme of things Allah occupies the centre stage. Not only has He created man, He has conferred upon him the best mould and guided him to the way of good and perfection. He has invested man with the potentials to attain perfection. As to man's nature, the Qur'ān observes: 'And follow you the constitution of Allah according to which He has constituted mankind and let there be no alteration in Allah's creation. That is the true faith.' (al-Rūm 30:30) It is stated in a *ḥadīth* that Allah has fashioned man in His mould, which points to the exalted status enjoyed by man. In the following verse reference is made to the best mould in which man is created: 'He has created the heavens and the earth in just proportion, and has given you shape, and has fashioned you in a comely shape, and to Him is the return.' (al-Taghābun 64:3) Since man has been created in the best mould, he should follow a lofty ideal in his life. Outward beauty should match inner excellence. Man cannot take lightly the purpose of his life. His only objective should be to draw closer to Allah in that it represents his ultimate destination. Allah being the source of all that is the best should be one's only goal and all efforts should be directed at winning His pleasure. Seeking His pleasure is a noble goal in itself and the means to earning His reward: 'Allah has promised the believing men and women Gardens under which rivers flow, wherein they shall abide, and goodly dwellings in the Everlasting Gardens and good-will from Allah is the greatest blessings of all. That is the supreme achievement.' (al-Tawbah 9:72)

Man's only objective should be gaining nearness to the Supreme and absolute being of Allah. Accordingly, the Islamic stance on morals is that man should abide by divine directives in every sphere of life. Islam pointedly asks man to follow the way of Allah. It should not be misconstrued in the sense of suppressing one's natural urges. Nor should one mistakenly hold that Islamic laws are a restriction imposed from without. Had there been a conflict between the way of Allah and human nature, the above proposition could be entertained. Since Allah has created man in the natural way, no coercion is involved in directing him to follow His way. For it amounts to acting in line with one's own nature. As long as man abides by Allah's way he fulfils his natural urges. Furthermore, on gaining gnosis of Allah man attains self-knowledge. This facilitates his adherence to morals.

Having identified Allah as the source of man's pivotal concern Islam directs man to emulate the divine attributes in his word and deed so that he is imbued with His hue: 'Ours is the dye of

Allah and who is better at dyeing than Allah? And we are His worshippers.' (al-Baqarah 2:138) Man is obliged to worship Him and adhere to His directives in every sphere of activity. Divine attributes should be reflected, no matter however faintly, in our conduct, for it is the divine attributes that invest our life with meaning and purpose, and instruct us in perennial values. Neglect of those values leads to life-in-death. Reflection on and responsiveness to the divine attributes enable man to ascertain His will. As a result, one is in a better position to follow His way and rise to higher ranks in His sight. The Qur'ān brings home the above point thus: 'For those who believe not in the Hereafter is an evil similitude, and to Allah applies the sublime similitude, and He is the Mighty, the Wise.' (al-Naḥl 16:60) As Allah is sublime, His servants should not be in a miserable condition. For He is their Custodian and Patron. However, if man severs his ties with Allah and prefers for himself a path culminating in wretchedness, he himself is responsible for his misery. Allah invites man to a way of life that guarantees an eternal, joyful life. The wicked, however, who fail to appreciate this and are wholly given to this world, deprive themselves of the rewards promised by Allah. Although their Lord is All-Mighty and All-Wise they prefer a life of ignorance and disgrace. Accordingly one can help them achieve deliverance.

In Islam the full range of human action is subject to its moral code. Accordingly, moral order occupies the pride of place. One of the objectives of the Prophet's mission was to instruct mankind in morals. He declared: 'I have been sent down in order to complete the best moral standards' (*al-Muwaṭṭa*'). The moral system in Islam takes into account all relevant points and does not suffer any gaps. Moral thought is concerned, in the main, with the following: (i) identifying excellence in morals (ii) imparting such knowledge so as to distinguish between good and evil and right and wrong (iii) and urging those incentives that prompt one to do good.

In Islam the highest felicity is to win the pleasure of Allah. It is the pivot around which all our activities should revolve. Accomplishing what Allah demands of us is the ultimate objective of one's life. The pursuit of this goal keeps one away from all error in this life. More importantly, one can fulfill all one's needs and desires while striving for this goal. The *Sharī'ah* accommodates all the natural human needs and urges. Islam accords priority to the values of justice, love, regard for others, truth and beauty. Needless to say, all these values are inter-linked and complementary. Taken together they represent a whole. Islam recognizes the worth of each value and accords it a suitable place. Since to a degree, these values reflect divine attributes, they contribute to the construction of an ideal society. In the light of these values, one can easily distinguish between good and evil. To put it in summary form – seeking the pleasure of Allah sets the standard for man to discern between right and wrong. The Qur'ān directs man to be generous, as Allah has been kind and generous to him (al-Qaṣaṣ 28:77). Doing good to others is thus the best way for man in that it is closer to the divine norm. Any path other than this entails disorder and corruption. The Qur'ān categorically forbids the causing of corruption. It is plainly stated at many places in the Qur'ān that Allah does not approve of those who cause corruption. *Aḥadīth* clarify that Allah, being lenient, prefers leniency and forbearance. It is evident from several Qur'ānic passages and *aḥadīth* that divine attributes stand out as a beacon of light to guide moral conduct. Man instinctively discriminates between good and evil and he is naturally drawn to appreciate good and to abhor evil. The Qur'ān therefore describes virtues and vices as reputable and disreputable deeds respectively. The Prophet (peace and blessings be upon him) observed: 'Righteousness is good morality and wrongdoing is that which wavers in your soul and which you dislike people finding out about.' (Muslim) It goes without saying that the Prophet's observations are always in line with human nature.

There are many factors that prompt one to do good. Of these, the first and foremost is to win Allah' pleasure. In comparison to it, other factors are only secondary and complement the above-mentioned main consideration.

Hallmarks of the Islamic moral system

It will be worthwhile here to outline some hallmarks of the Islamic moral system:

1. The Islamic moral code is based on certain unalterable principles, which do not admit any amendment. Moral values as envisioned by Islam are constant and consistent, as they are not prescribed by an imperfect mind. On the contrary, this moral code is legislated by Allah Who is free from any lapse and Who is fully aware of all the needs of man.

2. This system does not demand reform only in an individual's personal life. Rather, it seeks to transform the entire collective social life. Morals govern each and every aspect of human life. No sphere of human activity or relationship falls outside the constraints of the moral principle.

3. This system is based on benevolence that seeks perfection. Since perfection is a positive, creative feature, the whole moral edifice is adorned with this feature.

The sense of benevolence that we acquire from divine attributes consists of other elements as well, such as authority, justice, truth, beauty, mercy, compassion, eternity and coherence.

Life and growth

The Islamic concept promotes the growth of goodness. In this sense it is evolutionary. However, Islam is not concerned merely with material life, which is transient and ephemeral. Rather, it focuses attention on life after death. In pursuance of this aim it directs man to draw upon values that are life-enriching and constant. The life after death promised by Islam transcends the constraints of space and time. One can grasp it only with the help of intuition. The Qur'ān directs: 'Do not regard those slain in the way of Allah as dead. Nay, they are alive with their Lord and get their sustenance.' (Āl 'Imrān 3:169) As Allah is eternal, those adhering to His way are likely to be blessed with eternal life. Disregard for His way will nevertheless result in annihilation and eternal torment. Life has boundless potentials. It is natural for man to strive for better and to keep himself engaged in that effort.

Beauty and truth

In the Islamic value system beauty and truth are of prime importance. The Prophet (peace and blessings be upon him) said: 'Allah is beautiful and He loves beauty.' Beauty is related to man's both inward and outward being. The Qur'ān informs that beauty is an absolute and universal aesthetic value which gives delight and tranquillity. In the divine being it appears at its most vivid. 'To Him belong the most beautiful names.' (Ṭā Hā 20:8) Allah is characterized with the best features. Islam seeks to infuse beauty and purpose in man's deeds and morals. This can be achieved only when one's deeds aim at pleasing Allah. What is theoretically termed beauty is the moral sense in its perceptible form. Beauty does not stand in this context for something alluring and deceptive. It reflects truth in the highest degree. As already indicated, all moral values are intrinsically related to one another. Whatever is removed from truth lacks beauty.

Knowledge and vision

Allah's knowledge is all-embracing. He, therefore, does not keep man ignorant. The Qur'ān demands of man his adherence to morals. This calls for knowledge. Man is exhorted to overcome his blind conformity to convention and superstition. The Qur'ān declares that Allah being the patron of believers takes them away from darkness into light. Elsewhere it states: 'Is he who was dead and We revived him, and appointed for him a light with which he walks among mankind, like him

58

who is in darkness from which he cannot emerge?' (al-An'ām 6:122)

Power and authority

These are unmistakably Divine attributes and man should not disregard them. A moral system, not supported by the power and authority needed for its implementation can, at best, be an exhortation to do good. It cannot really succeed in rescuing people from the morass in which they are bound. This truth is expressed in the Qur'ānic verse: 'Say: "O Allah, sovereign of the Dominion. You give dominion to whom You will, and You take away dominion from whom You will. You exalt whom You will, and You abase whom You will. And in Your hand is the good, and surely You are potent over everything."' (Āl 'Imrān 3:26) The 'good' referred to in the above supplication, stands for power and authority. The All-Mighty is expected to bless His devout servants with power and authority.

Justice and equity

Justice is another of the eminent divine attributes. Establishing justice, therefore, is a prominent feature of the Islamic moral system. Believers are obliged to practise justice in every sphere of life, and give justice to friends and foes alike. Its other ramifications are the regard for treaties, and the observance of justice and truth and equity. The Prophet (peace and blessings be upon him) said: 'One who is not trustworthy is devoid of faith. One who does not abide by an agreement lacks faith.'

Mercy and love

Without mercy and love a moral system tends to be mechanical and cold. Love invests life with joy, charm and colour. That Allah is Most Merciful is a recurrent Qurʾānic affirmation. It is declared unequivocally that He is the Bestower, full of love. This calls for mutual love and understanding among men. It means, beyond acting with love towards one's near and dear ones, to have an overflowing love for all of mankind. Those in more need deserve more of concern and love, which should be extended equally to one's acquaintances, neighbours, wayfarers and mankind in general.

A unified whole

As already pointed out, the Islamic moral system stands out as a unified whole, comprising all the values. Furthermore, these are geared towards a single objective, which dictates one's deeds. As a result, moral life reflects the unity of purpose.

What prompts man to do good

An important issue when discussing morals is to ascertain the factors that motivate one to do good. In Islam, winning Allah's pleasure is the prime factor, both a natural and very strong incentive, and one that by its very nature is unalterable. A sane person stands out above others by his urge to seek Allah's pleasure. He is not distracted in the least in performing his duties lest it might provoke divine displeasure. This does not imply that Islam dismisses other factors, but those are to be seen as complementary and supplementary. We should not lose sight of this order of priority. (Some of the supplementary factors will be discussed below.)

One's realization and appreciation of Allah's innumerable favours fill the heart with overflowing gratitude to Him. This motivates good deeds and obedience to Him. Islam therefore regards it as the very basis of faith: 'Why would Allah afflict you with torment, if you return thanks and believe?' (al-Nisā' 4:147) Gratitude is thus an important driving force. The grateful servants of Allah find it gratifying to obey Him. The Qur'ān therefore highlights this point: 'Say: "He it is Who has brought you forth and has endowed you with hearing and sight and heart. Little thanks it is you give."' (al-Mulk 67:23)

One who is concerned about the Hereafter cannot neglect his obligations. What accounts in the main, for man's negligence is that he leads life without any attention to his ultimate end. The Qur'ān repeatedly draws attention to this truth so that man may overcome his negligence and forgetfulness. For example, addressing those lost in negligence, the Qur'ān asks: 'Nay; you prefer the life of this world whereas the Hereafter is far better and more lasting.' (al-A'lā 87:16-17) The life Hereafter is eternal whereas the present one is ephemeral. Man is in a position to improve his prospects in the life to come, provided his conduct is exemplary and he embraces faith.

Man's conscience constantly urges him to do good and accept true faith. The Qur'ān illustrates the point thus: 'There are many signs on earth and in man's own being for those who have conviction. Will you not reflect?' (al-Dhāriyāt 51:20-21)

If man acts on reason, he will realize that he should not lag behind in doing good. The Qur'ān makes this point in its inimitable style: 'Do you enjoin good deeds on others while you disregard yourselves though you recite the Book. Will you not [act on] reason?' (al-Baqarah 2:44) Man instinctively seeks to derive benefit and avoid loss. This is commonplace. While drawing upon this natural response of man the Qur'ān observes: 'Say: Shall we declare to you the greatest losers in respect of their deeds? They are those whose effort is wasted in the life of the world, and they imagine that they are doing well in action.' (al-Kahf 18:103-104) At another place it is stated in the Qur'ān: '[Nuḥ said:] Beg forgiveness of your Lord. He is ever Most Forgiving. He will send down upon you rains copiously. And He will increase you in riches and will bestow on you Gardens and will bestow on you rivers. What ails you that you look not for majesty in Allah?' (Nūḥ 71:10-13).

It is natural on man's part to compete with others. The Qur'ān invokes this natural urge of surpassing others in asking man to excel others in doing good: 'And had Allah so willed, He would have made you all a single community, but He willed it not, in order that He may try you by what He has given you. Race (compete) therefore to virtues.' (al-Mā'idah 5:48) Similarly, 'Strive with one another in hastening towards forgiveness from your Lord and towards a Garden of which the width is as the width of the heavens and the earth.' (al-Ḥadīd 57:21)

Man's sense of shame is also a powerful stimulant. The Qur'ān refers to it in order to motivate man in the cause of good: 'And what ails you that you do not fight in the way of Allah and for the oppressed among men and women and children who say: "Our Lord! Take us from this town the people of which are ungodly, and raise for us from You a friend and appoint for us from You a helper."' (al-Nisā' 4:75) The aesthetic sense is also a help in avoiding a life of stagnation and degeneration – it motivates good conduct so that it reflects decorum and beauty. It is important that these qualities are inward as well as outward. The Prophet (peace and blessings be upon him) made it plain that an outward beauty devoid of good conduct was worthless. He used to make the supplication: 'O Allah! Improve my conduct as You have adorned me outwardly.' The Qur'ānic affirmation that Allah has created man in the best mould (al-Tīn 95:4) if properly understood, motivates one to seek excellence. The desire for calm and tranquillity and for perfecting the self are other important motivators for doing good, as stated in the Qur'ān: [see al-Ra'd 13:28, al-'Alā 87:14, and al-Shams 91:9-10].

CHAPTER 3

Self-development: Importance, Prerequisites, Methodology and Modern Challenges

Abdur Rashid Siddiqui

THE BASIC REQUISITES FOR *TAZKIYAH*

There is a way to accomplish a task that is the right way to do it. Unless one possesses the necessary skills and knowledge, the task cannot be accomplished efficiently. A well-known Persian saying states: 'Whatever the wise man does, so too does the fool, but after a great deal of damage.' To avoid such damage it is essential that one should first gain necessary information about how the work should be accomplished.

Human resource is a basic requisite for the success of an organization. There must be trained, competent people in the organization, always striving to expand its activities. It is on account of the importance of training that self-development and self-purification occupy pride of place in the writings on Islam. Since our faith embraces all spheres of human activity, our training programme should be multi-faceted and comprehensive.

Tazkiyah

The core objective of the training is the attainment of self-purification. The term *tazkiyah* carries the two meanings of 'purifying' and 'facilitating growth'. The two are inter-related in that what is free of impurity, corruption and evil is bound to flourish naturally. The purification accomplished by the Messengers of Allah carried both elements. They purged the hearts of people of evil, especially their immoral acts, and also they helped their moral sense to blossom and develop. Indeed, the purification of mankind is one of the important objectives for which the messengers were sent. This is explicit in the Qur'ān's account of the objectives of the Prophet Muḥammad's mission: 'It is He Who sent among the unlettered ones a Messenger from among themselves, reciting to them His verses, purifying them, and teaching them the Book and Wisdom. And they had been before in manifest error.' (al-Jumu'ah 62:2) Man's abiding success consists in his exercising self-restraint, especially controlling the base desires of the self and pursuing the way of goodness and virtue: 'By the soul and Him Who perfected it in proportion; then He inspired it with conscience of what is wrong for it and what is right for it. Indeed he succeeds who purifies his own self. And indeed he fails who corrupts his own self.' (al-Shams 91:7-10) Almost the same truth features in another Qur'ānic assertion: 'He attains success who purifies himself.' (al-A'lā 87:14)

Thus, man's deliverance and success are contingent upon his self-purification. Every day the caller to prayer invites Muslims five times a day to attain success by way of doing prayers. This confirms prayer as one of the means for self-purification. Allah will grant us success in our striving for purification on account of such acts.

The Basic requisites for *tazkiyah*

Having noted the importance and relevance of self-purification, we shall now identify its basic requisites – without which one cannot succeed in the effort to attain self-purification:

1. INTENTION AND COMMITMENT

One of the best known of *aḥādīth* (cited in Bukhārī and Muslim) teaches that actions will be weighed in terms of their intention. One must therefore make it a point to purify one's intention. Doing so is an important priority for *tazkiyah*. Unless the person sincerely intends to reform himself, Allah does not enable him to do so. The intent to reform is followed by commitment to that goal. If the intent to seek self-purification is sound, then as the person commits himself to self-reform, he is helped and sustained by Allah.

In his work *Tazkiyah-e-Nafs* Mawlānā Amīn Aḥsan Iṣlāḥī observes:

If one is not fully committed to self reform, even the best guidance cannot avail him. There is no better guidebook than the Qurʾān. However, it benefits only those who resolve to act upon its guidance. It does not do any good to those who praise its eloquence or other literary excellence, but are not prepared to act upon its guidance. The term *murīd* in the parlance of *taṣawwuf* refers, in my opinion to one who is committed to reforming his self. He is ready to face every hardship, make every sacrifice and lay down his life and wealth in this cause. One lacking this commitment is not a true *murīd*. (p. 12)

The Prophet's Companions were ardent to attain self-purification. This comes across most clearly in the incident related to 'Abdullāh ibn Maktūm, recorded in 'Abasa 80:9-10. It is pointedly said by Allah in verse 3 of this *sūrah* that 'Abdullāh, a blind man made an effort to join the Prophet's company in order to grow in virtue, to achieve self-purification.

Let us be clear at this point that an individual may want to acquire many things. However, the desire to have something does not necessarily represent the intent to obtain it. As the proverb says: 'If wishes were horses, beggars would ride' – wishful thinking does not lead one to the wished-for end.

Lack of determination is a fundamental human weakness. Allah refers to it: 'And indeed We made a covenant with Adam before, but he forgot, and We found on his part no firm will-power.' (Ṭā Hā 20:115) Because this want of will-power is innate in human beings, one should be constantly on guard against it, and steadfastly pursue one's goal.

2. Understanding the requisites

The importance and excellence of knowledge are explicitly stated in the Qur'ān and the *Ḥadīth*. Reference to knowledge features in the early verses of the Qur'ān. The first word revealed to the Prophet (peace and blessings be upon him) is '*Iqrā*' which means to recite or read. Likewise, knowledge (not given to the angels) was the foremost bounty granted to the Prophet Adam (peace be upon him). A human being stands superior to all the creatures of the universe by dint of his knowledge. According to a *ḥadīth*, one is obliged to seek knowledge. In his *Ṣaḥīḥ al-Bukhārī*, Imām Bukhārī has assigned knowledge a place next only to revelation and faith. Imām al-Ghazālī opens his work *Iḥyāʾ al-ʿUlūm al-Dīn* with a discussion of knowledge, divided into seven parts. Without knowledge one cannot gain any understanding of the basic requisites of self-purification, and without developing that understanding one cannot overcome weaknesses and lapses.

Reading alone does not suffice for developing and understanding faith or attaining knowledge. Unless the person acts on what he knows, his knowing by itself cannot benefit him. The Prophet's Companions did not proceed further until they had assimilated the message of ten verses recited to them by the Prophet (peace and blessings be upon him), in both their mind and action. In this way, they gained both theoretical and practical knowledge of the Qurʾān at the same time. Ḥasan al-Baṣrī remarks: 'Learning something and acting upon it is better than all the bounties of the world.' *Aḥādīth* speak highly of knowledge that benefits man and which is reflected in his actions.

Experts on psychology tell us that we remember only 10% of what we read, 20% of what we see, 50% of what we see and hear, 80% of what we say and 90% of what we say and do. Practical efforts are therefore essential. There is a famous saying: 'Tell me, I forget. Show me, I remember. Involve me, I understand.'

3. CONSTANT STRIVING

After making a firm commitment and gaining the requisite knowledge, it is imperative to devote oneself wholeheartedly to the cause. Supplications are, of course, important. However, supplications, not followed up by practical steps, do not result in some miracle. Man cannot attain any success without effort and constant striving. The Qur'ān clarifies: '... man can have nothing but what he strives for.' (al-Najm 53:39) It is worth mentioning that one should not merely complete a formality. Rather, one should try his level best, taking no chance. Allah makes this point about man's intention and commitment: 'And whoever desires the Hereafter and strives for it with due effort, and being a believer – those are the ones whose striving will be appreciated.' (al-Isrā' 17:19)

Almost the same point is made about struggle (*Jihād*). For Muslims are directed to undertake it in the manner befitting it.

4. REALIZATION OF THE IDEAL

Our main ideal is to achieve Allah's pleasure and gain success in the Hereafter. We must never lose sight of this goal. Obviously there are numerous obstructions in the way of this goal. Our approach should be like the progress of a river flowing on to merge with the sea. High mountains do not deter it from flowing on further – rather than striking vainly against rocks and thus dissipating its energy, it finds a new path in order to move consistently towards its destination. A true understanding of the ideal and a keen desire to achieve it act as an impetus, urging man all the time to keep on.

5. HIGH STANDARDS

We should learn how to accomplish our task in the best, the most befitting, manner. Likewise, we should devote ourselves heart and soul to our assignment. The Prophet (peace and blessings be upon him) draws attention to this in his observation: 'Allah loves those who do their job perfectly.' (Bayhaqī) In Islamic terminology it is called '*iḥsān*'. The Prophet (peace and blessings be upon him) defines it thus: 'Worship Allah in the manner as if you were seeing Him. If that is not possible [for you] be mindful that He sees you.' (Muslim) This standard of *iḥsān* should be observed in all affairs of life, be these acts of worship or mutual dealings. Every *imām* reminds us of the same in his Friday sermon: 'Allah orders you to act with justice and *Iḥsān*.' (al-Naḥl 16:90) Allah accepts those deeds that are performed sincerely and perfectly.

6. DAILY ROUTINE

An effort should be made to make self-purification the axis around which our life revolves. It should not be relegated to the margins. Training programmes may be helpful, but they cannot replace our conscious effort to seek self-purification. Our understanding and skills are no doubt enhanced for the time being by our participation in training programmes. However, what is needed is that this desire for self-purification should be fully imbibed by us, and become an intrinsic part of our being. The sole objective of the acts of worship prescribed by Allah is that we may purify ourselves.

7. INVOKING AND ESTABLISHING TIES WITH ALLAH

The objective of self-purification is that a person develops and strengthens his relationship with Allah. All righteous persons have consistently urged their companions to reinforce their relationship with Allah. The stronger this relationship is the more consistent and committed one will be in thought and deed. Love for Allah is the impetus that enables one not to deviate from the straight path even in the most adverse circumstances. The desire to meet Allah and the consciousness of answerability in the Hereafter fill a person with both hope and fear, and urge him on to his destination. As to our relationship with Allah, whether it is growing or weakening, Mawlānā Mawdūdī significantly observed:

> To ascertain this, you need not wait for some vision, miracle or supernatural spectacle. Allah has placed its measure in every heart. You can measure it at any time. You should take stock of your life, your activities and your responses. You should ask of yourself, how far you are sincere to the covenant that you have made with Allah by embracing faith. (*Taḥrīk Awr Kārkun*, p. 155)

It goes without saying that a person cannot accomplish anything without Allah's help and support. Those who opt for the way of obedience to Allah are constantly tested. The Qur'ān makes this point at several places, for example: 'Do people think that they will be left alone because they say: "We believe", and will not be tested? And We indeed tested those who were before them and Allah will certainly make it known those who are true and will certainly make it known those who are liars.' (al-'Ankabūt 29:2-3)

We will be tested in order to ascertain whether we are sincere believers or hypocrites. After having undergone these tests and trials we will be blessed with Allah's help and support. We should therefore keep on unceasingly petitioning Him for His help and support. According to Mawlānā Amīn Aḥsan Islāḥī, it is implicit in *Sūrah al-Fātiḥah* that one cannot succeed in the intention of serving Allah unless the ability to do so is granted by Him.

8. STOCK-TAKING AND SOUL-SEARCHING

Notwithstanding a person's grand plans and painstaking efforts in the way of truth and striving for self-reform, he is distracted by the base desires of the self, Satan's instigations, worldliness, societal pressure and family considerations and numerous other interests. These can shake even a committed believer, so that he feels himself powerless in the face of these distractions and pressures. However, wishful thinking cannot help him reach the destination. He should regularly do stock-taking and soul-searching, review his actions and motives, regret his mistakes, and try anew. Notwithstanding the unpleasant nature of this self-assessment, it is the only means for alerting a person in time and guiding him to the straight path. It is reported in a *ḥadīth* that the Prophet (peace and blessings be upon him) sought Allah's forgiveness more than seventy times a day. He always turned to Him to pardon his lapses. This stock-taking is imperative in that it prepares a person mentally for his accountability in the Hereafter: 'Take stock of your deeds before you are called to account' is a precious piece of admonition and advice.

SELF-DEVELOPMENT AND ITS METHODOLOGY

What are the practical steps to be taken on the way to self-development and self-purification? What is to be the starting point? What should the means be to self-reform? Answers to these questions hold the key to the door to self-development and self-purification. Some of the relevant important points are discussed below.

1. PURIFYING THE HEART

Self-purification starts with purifying one's heart. The heart is mentioned again and again in both the Qur'ān and the *Ḥadīth*. Of course, this usage does not refer literally to the bodily organ enabling blood circulation. Rather, it is a metaphor for a person's whole being, his personality and character, his psychological make-up, his desires, and his mental and emotional inclinations which prompt him to do certain things and to avoid others. It is well defined by Khurram Murad in his *How to Attain Self-development*:

> What you need for attaining every goal is your own personality. The expression personality is used here in its broadest sense. Included in it are your body, your mind, your abilities, your heart, your emotions, your character and your morals. Your personality is the sum of all. (*Tarjumān al-Qur'ān*, November 1996, p. 26)

The Qur'ān describes thus the role of the heart in a person's ultimate success: 'The Day whereon neither wealth nor sons will avail, except him who brings to Allah a clean heart.' (al-Shu'arā' 26:88-89) In view of the importance of the heart the Prophet

73

(peace and blessings be upon him) observed: 'Beware! There is a lump of flesh in the human body. If it is sound, it ensures the soundness of the whole body. However, if it is corrupt, it corrupts the whole body. Truly it is the heart.' (Bukhārī and Muslim) The Qur'ān pointedly identifies the heart as the root cause of evil in man (al-Baqarah 2:10). All evils arise from the 'blindness' of the heart: 'Verily, it is not the eyes that grow blind but it is the hearts which are in the breast that grow blind.' (al-Ḥajj 22:46) Therefore, the starting point of self-purification should be the cleansing of the heart. It can help one attain success. The Prophet (peace and blessings be upon him) said: 'He certainly achieves success whose heart is reserved exclusively by Allah for faith and who is granted a clean heart.' (Aḥmad and Bayhaqī) We must understand that man is not consistent in his responsiveness, and therefore needs to supplicate continually that he may remain always on the straight path. He should constantly pray to Allah: 'Our Lord! Do not let our hearts deviate now after You have guided us.' (Āl 'Imrān 3:8) It was the Prophet's practice to make this supplication: 'O One Who transforms the hearts! Make our hearts steady in the cause of Your faith.' (Ibn Mājah and Aḥmad)

2. REMEMBRANCE OF ALLAH AND ACTS OF WORSHIP

One's heart should always be filled with the remembrance of Allah. Forgetfulness and negligence are the main weaknesses of human beings. The only remedy is that the believer should develop God-consciousness and be constantly aware He watches him. All acts of worship aim at drawing man closer to Allah. The Qur'ān says: 'Establish prayers for My remembrance.' (Ṭā Hā 20:14) The Friday sermon too, constitutes the commands and remembrance of Allah (al-Jumuʿah 62:10). But we must be clear that the remembrance of Allah is not restricted to certain acts of formal worship. The point is that one should always remember Him: 'Those who remember Allah, standing, sitting and lying on their sides.' (Āl ʿImrān 3:191) Thābit Banānī (may Allah have mercy on him) once exclaimed: 'I know when my Lord remembers me.' Upon hearing this, those present trembled in fear and asked him how he knew this. In response he recited from verse 152 of *al-Baqarah*: 'Remember Me. I will remember you.' It is recorded in *ḥadīth qudsī*: 'I come up to the expectations of My servant. I am with him when he remembers Me. When he makes mention of Me in his heart, I make mention of him to Myself. When he mentions Me in a gathering, I mention him in a better gathering (of the angels).' (Bukhārī and Muslim)

It is the height of felicity for a human being that Allah remembers him and mentions him in the blessed gathering of the angels.

We have taken note of the importance and blessed nature of the remembrance of Allah. By the same token, one's neglect of it is fatal, bringing disgrace upon oneself. Those who forget Allah are forgotten by Him (al-Tawbah 9:67). Allah then lets them wander in the web of their own self (al-Ḥashr 59:19). One's disregard for Allah culminates in the ruin of the self.

It is worthy of note that everything in the universe is preoccupied with remembering and glorifying Allah. This point is explicitly made in the first verse of *Sūrah al-Ḥadīd* (chapter 57) and in many other places in the Qur'ān. As one is engaged in remembering, praising and glorifying Allah, he becomes at one with the entire universe. It opens the gate for all goodness and success for him.

The remembrance of Allah should permeate one's life in every respect. It should not be restricted to reciting certain formulas in privacy at an appointed hour. Prayers, *zakāh*, fasting and *ḥajj* are the practical manifestations of remembering Allah. Moreover, the remembrance of Allah is not confined to utterance and speech – one's whole mind and process of thinking should be constantly imbued with it, as the Qur'ān teaches: 'They reflect deeply about the creation of the heavens and earth, saying: "Our Lord! You have not created all this without purpose. Glory to You. Give us salvation from the torment of the Fire."' (Āl 'Imrān 3:191) Only that remembrance of Allah is most rewarding which involves our thoughts and prompts us to think about our answerability in the Hereafter. This in turn, motivates the measures needed to protect oneself against hellfire.

Besides acts of worship, study of the Qur'ān is another effective means for remembering Allah. Allah speaks of the Qur'ān itself as Remembrance (al-Anbiyā' 21:50 and al-Ḥijr 15:9). It is further said: 'And We have indeed made the Qur'ān easy to understand and remember; then is there anyone who will receive admonition?' (al-Qamar 54:17) One should recite the Qur'ān with utmost devotion and reflect over its contents.

Other modes of remembering Allah are reciting the supplications recorded on the Prophet's authority. These constantly remind one at every stage of life that one should turn wholly to Allah and maintain a close relationship with Him. These supplications should not be merely uttered – they should be reflected in one's thoughts and actions. The Qur'ān says: 'O you who believe! When you meet an enemy force, take a firm stand against them and remember the name of Allah much so that you may be successful.' (al-Anfāl 8:45) The point here is that constant remembrance of Allah facilitates one's engagement in *Jihād*.

The Qur'ān further states: 'O you who believe! Let not your properties or your children divert you from the remembrance of Allah, for whosoever does that, then they are the losers. And spend in charity of that with which We have provided you before death comes to one of you.' (al-Munāfiqūn 63:9-10) In this context, the remembrance of Allah consists in spending in His cause. One of the benefits of remembering Allah is that man is always mindful that he will die, and so spends generously for the sake of pleasing Allah.

The objective of all the prescribed duties of worship is to train us – training to prepare against and to remedy human weaknesses. One can attain the goal of self-purification by fulfilling these duties properly. Forgetfulness is a major weakness of man, the effective remedy for it is prayer. Man is liable to be swayed by the glitter of worldly life; he is drawn to amass wealth and may develop a strong love for it – the remedy for this is *zakāh* and spending for the pleasure of Allah in His cause. Similarly, man is vulnerable to the base desires of the self. He is gratified by eating, drinking, living to excess in luxury and indulging his lower appetites – the remedy lies in fasting, which trains and disciplines these appetites and desires. *Ḥajj* too, cures man of these weaknesses because its rituals effectively prefigure the proceedings of the Day of Judgement.

3. FRATERNITY, COMPANIONSHIP AND THE COMPANY OF THE RIGHTEOUS

The way to self-purification is burdened with numerous obstacles and hardships. The individual cannot pursue this way steadily on his own. However, like-minded companions may help him reach his destination, in spite of the obstacles, distractions and hindrances of the way. Companionship helps one overcome hardships and boosts one's morale. In adverse circumstances, the valour and consistency displayed by others inspire one greatly. The Qur'ān therefore speaks of believing men and women as each other's companions (al-Tawbah 9:71). Elsewhere it extols the entire Muslim community as a single brotherhood (al-Ḥujurāt 49:10). Since Muslims share the same beliefs, their relations should be characterized by mutual love and sympathy. They should be bound to one another by the ties of mercy and fraternity. The Qur'ān pointedly says that the believers are kind to one another. Fraternity is hailed as an essential requisite of faith in *aḥādīth*. The Prophet (peace and blessings be upon him) is on record as remarking: 'You cannot be true believers unless you love one another.' (Muslim)

The importance of like-minded companions is best appreciated in the light of Allah's counsel to the Prophet (peace and blessings be upon him): 'And bear yourself patiently with those who call on their Lord morning and afternoon, seeking His face, and let not your eyes overlook them.' (al-Kahf 18:28).

It is likely that at times one may have to forge ties outside the family, in preference to one's near and dear ones. Although initially hard this is essential for training the self.

Shaikh Sa'dī's remarks about the benefits of the company of the righteous are apt. He says that one who is seeking the way of virtue should join the company of the righteous. Modern experts in sociology and psychology are unanimous that the influence of one's companions on one's morals and manners is decisive.

The Prophet (peace and blessings be upon him) said that one's faith and way of life reflect the influence of his companions. One should therefore exercise caution in choosing his friends and companions.

In his influential work *Kashf al-Maḥjūb* Shaikh 'Alī al-Hujwīrī records the following anecdote: 'A man was performing *ṭawāf* (circumambulation) of the Ka'bah and was praying repeatedly: "O Allah! Make my brothers and friends virtuous." When asked why he did not pray for himself at such a blessed site, he replied: "I will return to my brothers and friends. If they turn into virtuous persons, I too, will become righteous in their company. However, if they are wicked and evil, I will adopt the same habits under their influence."'

4. DA'WAH

The most effective means to attain knowledge is to engage in teaching. The one engaged in imparting knowledge must, naturally, reflect upon it to improve his own understanding and insights. By the same token, conveying the message to others, which we reckon as the best for ourselves and which we consistently follow, is the natural way for self-training. One need not retire to some monastery and engage in contemplation for this purpose. His own surroundings and the company of his friends serve as his training ground. Although the objective of the call is to convey the message to others, it motivates one to attain self-reform. Mawlānā Mawdūdī brings home this truth in his characteristically insightful manner:

> One of the features of preaching truth is that those engaged in it are imbued with the truth that they preach. The more one is actively engaged in preaching, in publicizing truth, in looking for the avenues for its promotion, for identifying arguments in support of it and for removing the obstructions on the way, the more he is devoted to it. This preaching helps them in another way as well. When he asks others to surrender themselves wholly to Allah, to remove all duplicity and hypocrisy in their way of life and to extirpate all the traces of *Jāhilīyah* (ignorance), his addressees critically and closely examine his own way of life with a view to identifying his weaknesses. Many persons are thus preoccupied with reforming and perfecting him. He draws freely upon the hard work of his critics in that it contributes to his gaining perfection. (*Taḥrīk Awr Kārkun,* pp. 103-104)

It is evident from the above that the natural process for self-development is that one should engage wholeheartedly in *Da'wah* work. Once one is involved in it, he does not need further ('specialist') training. This alone can help him gain excellence.

5. COLLECTIVE LIFE AND CONSTRUCTIVE CRITICISM

As one takes on collective life responsibilities under the Islamic discipline, organizing abilities are boosted and facilitate ascent to higher standards. Of course the efforts of disparate individuals alone cannot bring about the revolution that Islam demands of us. Only an organized movement can bring about the change in society as a whole. This truth is recognized in the following *ḥadīth*: 'The Prophet (peace and blessings be upon him) said: I ask you to do the following which Allah has obliged me to perform — hearing and obeying, jihād, *hijrah* and jamā'ah (organization).' (Tirmidhī)

Both Qur'ān and *Ḥadīth* emphasize obedience. *Hijrah* and *Jihād* bring out the best in a Muslim's character and prepare him for the sacrifices needed in the cause of Allah. He can attain self-development as a member of the organized movement. The critical spirit should be kept alive in an organization so that the ailments which can afflict collective life can be addressed. On the importance of criticism and its relevance to collective life Mawlānā Mawdūdī says:

> Criticism identifies the failing promptly and emphasizes the need for its redress. In collective life criticism has the same importance in moral terms as cleanliness has in the physical world. As people grow indifferent to public hygiene and cleanliness and make no effort to clean their surroundings, it pollutes the atmosphere of the entire town and breeds many diseases. By the same logic, in the absence of criticism, a community, society or organization is liable to go astray. It will be then beyond any reform. (*Taḥrīk Awr Kārkun*, p. 106)

As an active member of an organized society one learns how to work with others in spite of divergence of opinion. It is natural that people should differ in their views, temperaments and strategies. However, instead of being misguided by egotistical notions people can collaborate and while respecting the courtesies of divergence of opinion, they can prevail over differences.

6. OBSTACLES AND PITFALLS

A responsible highways authority will erect a variety of warning signs in order to alert drivers to dangers and so ensure safe passage. Similarly it is necessary that certain of the obstacles in the path of self-purification be identified for the benefit of the seekers of truth. Doing so will help them reach their destination safely. In broad terms, there are certain failings which gradually separate one from one's goal against which it is well to be forewarned:

a. *Negligence and carelessness*

This is a very common failing. One is without doubt, drawn by nature towards a programme of self-reform, and may be granted some success. However, human beings are liable to forgetfulness and negligence. The Qur'ān repeatedly warns against becoming one of those who are negligent. It is important therefore to be fully on guard, to value greatly any success and thank Allah profusely for it so that one may be deserving of more of His bounties. Conversely a lack of appreciation, indifference and negligence results in the loss of all that Allah has granted. The Qur'ān says plainly of the Jews and Christians that they did not value their Scriptures and disregarded them; as a result they fell prey to mutual differences and strayed from the straight path (al-Mā'idah 5:13-14).

b. *Pride and arrogance*

The believer who turns his attention to self-purification, shuns misdeeds and practices the virtues, will grow in social prominence and respect. People will praise him for his integrity, gentleness and piety. As he succeeds in his efforts to attain piety and excellence, his virtues become the focus of attention. However, if he is not careful enough, he may fall into pride, and suffer from complacency and conceit, and a superiority complex may trouble him. We must recognize that it is a Satanic strategy to deceiving the believer. Satan fell from Divine grace on account of his pride. It is recorded that the Prophet (peace and blessings be upon him) said: 'One with even an iota of pride will not enter Paradise.' (Muslim)

To protect oneself against pride and arrogance one should not look to those who are inferior in knowledge and good deeds, but to those who occupy higher ranks in terms of piety, knowledge and gnosis of Allah. We should always remember that Allah has presented for us the role model of the illustrious conduct of the Messengers and Companions. On comparison with that model, we will always become aware of our inferiority to them. That will protect us from falling prey to pride and arrogance. Once man suffers from the delusion that he has attained excellence, it marks the starting point of his decline and decay. One should, therefore, seek refuge with Allah against this, lest one is deprived thereby of all that he has gained.

c. *Desire for perfection*

It is a person's natural desire to attain the zenith of achievement in the field of his choice. This ambition in itself is valuable. However, since a human being is fallible, he cannot maintain the same standard of excellence at all times. Some people are never satisfied with what they do, while also obsessed with the desire to achieve perfection. Failing to reach the highest standard, they lose heart and slide into despair and despondency. By definition an ideal is something to be pursued, it is in principle always unattainable. As already indicated, the Prophet represents the role model for us to emulate: it is the highest standard to which we cannot measure up.

d. *Hastiness*

Human beings are instinctively hasty (al-Anbiyā' 21:37), while the process of self-purification is long and drawn out. One cannot straightaway achieve what one wishes and wants in this respect, and is moreover exposed to many obstacles and hardships on the way. Perseverance and courage are needed to overcome these. Succumbing to impatience or hastiness is itself an impediment to success, whereas consistently and valiantly confronting the hardships and obstacles brings out the best in the seeker. Indeed, the striving and steadfastness are essential elements of self-purification. One cannot attain high standards by acting hastily and impatiently.

e. *Despair*

Despair is a fatal disease. At times it brings one into unbelief. Allah says: 'Never give up hope of Allah's mercy. Certainly no one despairs of Allah's mercy, except the people who disbelieve.' (Yūsuf 12:87) In adverse circumstances when the chances of success are remote, one is naturally inclined to lose hope and turn to cynicism or pessimism. However, even in the face of repeated failures one must never despair of Allah's mercy. Every failure should inspire renewed vigour to confront the unfavourable circumstances and persevere in the cause, in accordance with the promise of Allah: 'As for those who strive hard in Our cause, We will surely guide them to Our paths.' (al-'Ankabūt 29:69)

f. *Extremism*

Human beings are prone to go to extremes when overtaken by passion. They often adopt an extremist position on particular issues, whether acts of worship or points of morality, overemphasizing certain matters at the expense of others. Islam enjoins human beings to seek balance and moderation in their outlook and warns them against extremism of any sort. One should therefore observe moderation in the effort to attain self-purification. It is reported on the authority of Anas that the Prophet (peace and blessings be upon him) said: 'Do not strain yourself in matters of faith lest Allah may treat you harshly.' In another *ḥadīth* he warned: 'Beware! Do not become entrapped by extremism. For people before you were destroyed on account of their extremism in faith.'

We have taken note of the obstacles and pitfalls on the road to self-purification. This should not give rise to the impression that one cannot make progress on this road. Certainly this is not that difficult. Human beings instinctively welcome goodness and are repelled by evil. There are lessons to be learnt from every event in this universe, as well as from one's own experience. One does not stand in need of joining some training course to assimilate these lessons. Furthermore, it is within man's capacity to fulfill the obligations prescribed by Allah. Allah does not burden anyone beyond his capacity, for that would run counter to justice. Khurram Murad has discussed these matters in his *How to Attain Self-development*. Its study will therefore be beneficial.

MODERN MANAGEMENT TECHNIQUES FOR EFFECTIVE SELF-DEVELOPMENT

No organization can flourish without adequate and competent human resources. A commercial enterprise cannot succeed in its business without qualified personnel. So too, an Islamic movement which aims at social reform and social transformation cannot succeed in the absence of suitably qualified workers.

Everyone is obliged to arrange for his own self-development – if he is not willing, no one can do it for him. An organization can at most provide the infrastructure that may help individuals evaluate their skills and let them develop these. Every individual is unique and people have different abilities. Each differs from others in his genetic make-up, as in his fingerprints. This uniqueness is not restricted to man's physical form. His psychology, his mind, his temperament and his thinking processes differ sharply from those of others. We cannot mould everyone into the same pattern. However, they can be instructed alike and their thought patterns and conduct may be defined and channelled within certain limits. For example, if we ask them to assemble at a particular place, time and date, we should expect that they would turn up. Likewise, most of them are expected to make the sacrifices demanded of them, whether financial or otherwise. We should first ascertain what ability and expertise an organization requires in its workforce. Without this needs analysis, we cannot draw up a training programme.

1. RIGHTEOUSNESS

For the success of an Islamic movement it is imperative that the righteous persons be enlisted. They should be prepared to spend their wealth and other resources in this cause. Notwithstanding the social class to which they belong, if they are inclined towards truth, they may be trained and associated with the movement. Programmes may be drawn up for their intellectual, academic and moral development to strengthen their sincerity and righteousness of conduct. They may prove to be valuable assets for the movement. Well-trained and righteous persons are certainly essential for a religious movement, their help and support are its strength.

2. MANAGEMENT SKILLS

Management skills are badly needed in our times. Generally speaking, there is a dearth of resources. Our target therefore should be the optimum utilization of resources including time, and regularity and efficiency in our work. This can be achieved with the help of better planning, delegation of authority and time management. It has been established beyond doubt by recent studies and experiments that management skills make a big difference. This needs further discussion.

a. *Proper use of time*

Many of us complain that we have little time. On analyzing our daily routine, it emerges that this is only a pretext. For we waste time on unimportant things or resort to this pretext to cover up our inefficiencies.

Time is one of man's most precious assets. One may regain almost anything in life, but one cannot retrieve time. An important feature of time is that it should be utilized properly. It cannot be saved beyond a certain point. Let us realize that everyone is granted the same measure of time, the same twenty-four hours in a day. This perfect equality is not evident in any other divine bounty. Each of us will be called to account for all the bounties bestowed upon him. Of these, the most difficult to account for will be how we spent our time. In *Sūrah al-'Aṣr*, with reference to time fleeting by, our attention is drawn to these facts.

A proper organization and utilization of time aims to use one's own and others' time in the most effective way. First, each individual should take stock of how he spends his time. This should be followed by proper planning in order to accomplish everything in time. On stock-taking, it emerges that telephone conversations and dealing with visitors disturb schedules most. Then, there are many routine tasks, perhaps too many: on return from absence (holiday or illness) one is confronted with a backlog of work. Also, time is wasted in solving unexpected problems. Paperwork grows out of control. Meetings take up a lot of time. Then a large chunk of time is lost in perhaps unnecessary discussions. One is thus faced with many problems. An effective way to solving these is to start by compiling a list of them. One should record on a time-sheet how much time is spent on doing something, over a sufficient period – perhaps a few days. Then one should study the result in order to ascertain where time is being misspent and how this can be redressed. Obviously, it is hard to change established habits, but with the right commitment one can achieve anything. Another solution is to delegate authority properly and effectively. Below are some useful suggestions for addressing some of these problems.

b. *Time management*

Although people agree in principle to the need for time planning, they are apt to say that they do not have the time. The truth is that in the absence of planning one cannot have time for anything. Initially, some time must be spent on planning, but this is a useful investment. Since we have time in a limited measure, one must develop the habit of apportioning it wisely. This should be much easier for Muslims, as our prayer times already shape our day.

One should first draw up a list of tasks, short-term and long-term ones, and prioritize them. Long-term objectives may be sub-divided into practicable stages or targets, which can help maintain morale. There are many ways to attain a particular target, and it is important to decide the appropriate way in line with prevailing conditions. We have to take such decisions at every step in life. It is better to record in writing what we intend to do, as this helps focus on the goal and not get lost in distractions.

Our jobs are of two types: some are active, proceeding from our initiative, while others are essentially 're-active'. The former represent the real work in that they help us towards our goals. As to the latter, they are best illustrated by the unnecessary and irrelevant letters piling up on one's desk. Those who do not do good planning mistake the latter as the real work. It is therefore essential to exclude unnecessary items from one's list of tasks, items that obstruct one from the main goal. This will enable more time to be devoted to the active work, and an appropriate portion of time to be spent on the 'reactive' work.

A diary is essential for time planning. One should make a point of recording reports, jotting down the times of visits and meetings in the diary, so as to be informed of one's daily engagements. Besides a diary, a visual planner helps one keep track of monthly and annual engagements. One should regularly review one's schedules, as priorities can change when new issues arise, and one may have to adapt accordingly.

c. *Paperwork*

Most of our time is spent on reading reports or voluminous books. It is important to increase reading speed, which will help one read more in less time. This skill can be gained after a few weeks' practice. Scanning the introductory pages of books enables one to decide whether to read the whole book or not. As to letters and circulars received, one should divide these into the following three categories after looking at them: 1) those which need immediate action (out tray); 2) those on which some action may be necessary but not immediately (pending tray); 3) those on which others are to be consulted. Many irrelevant items are received in the mail which can be promptly thrown away. It will help one focus time on priority items. For unnecessary things will come to an end after a certain point of time.

d. *Meetings*

Much time is spent on meetings and gatherings. However, with the help of proper planning and meeting management, more work can be done in less time. Time can be saved if the participants bear in mind the following points: 1) They should have a considered opinion on the items on the agenda. 2) They should come to the meeting on time and bring the relevant papers. 3) They should make their points clearly and avoid unnecessary digressions. 4) They should participate courteously in the proceedings. 5) They should willingly accept the decisions taken at the meeting.

e. *Telephone*

The telephone is, no doubt, a necessity. However, if it is not properly used, it leads to much wastage of time. The following points should be observed regarding use of the telephone: 1) Be clear what is to be discussed with someone and if he is not present, what message is to be given to whom, and also prepare any message to be left on his answering machine. 2) It is preferable to note in writing the points to be discussed on the phone. 3) On receiving a call one should clearly state one's name. 4) If the call is for someone else, the message should be recorded and left for his attention. 5) If one is busy in work and does not want to attend the telephone, one should use an answering machine.

f. *Wasting others' time*

Most of us are guilty of wasting others' time. Some of the bad habits are: keeping people waiting, arriving late, replying late or failing to respond at all, being absent without a valid reason, interfering in matters which do not concern one, not listening to someone attentively or misconstruing it, forgetting important items and presenting one's problems before others with the insistence that these be solved.

To save our own and others' time, we should be guided by the Prophet's very pertinent advice: 'One of the qualities of a Muslim is that he disregards what does not concern him.' (Tirmidhī)

g. *Delegating authority*

This does not mean assigning those jobs to others that one hates to do oneself, or find dull and boring. It means that some authority should be delegated to colleagues to take appropriate decisions without further consultation, and be answerable for them. Before delegation in this way one should decide carefully what tasks can in principle be assigned to others. Here are some of the advantages of delegating authority: 1) one will be able to devote more time to more important jobs; 2) others will gain experience; 3) they will feel encouraged and confident; 4) and as they are held responsible, the job will be done in a better way.

However, before delegating authority, one needs to think hard and long about it: one learns how to do it after much experience. The following points may be helpful in this regard: 1) It is essential to select competent staff. The 'manager' should not blame incompetent staff for incompetent work as he (the manager) is responsible for the appointment of staff. Authority should be delegated only to competent persons. 2) Those entrusted with authority must be trained for it and in it. One should first work together with them and monitor their performance after delegating authority to them. They should be directed to submit reports, and suitable advice should be given to them. To begin with, relatively less important tasks may be entrusted to them, then gradually more difficult and sensitive assignments as their competence and confidence develops. 3) There should be regular contact both during and after this period of training. The authority delegated to others should be clearly spelled out. 4) Once authority is delegated, interference should be avoided. One should not immediately revoke the orders of a junior. When he calls for help, it may be better to direct him to think for himself and find a way out. This will help him find solutions to problems. 5) Delegation of authority is not synonymous with its abdication. It is essential that one reviews the work regularly and monitors its progress. It is important to supervise effectively even after delegating authority. It has been insightfully observed that one enjoys real authority when one delegates it to others.

3. COMMUNICATION SKILLS

One of the challenges of modern times is to communicate effectively, draw upon the available means of communication and gain the communicative skills that can be instrumental in presenting the call to truth. Much has been written on developing spoken and written skills of communication. At present, overhead projectors, power points, charts, and computer graphics are widely used for presentations, and these do enhance communicative skills.

a. *Video*

Training programmes may be produced on video to impart necessary skills to those engaged in *da'wah* work. Using role-play technique of presenting *da'wah* to people of various schools of thought and different abilities is very effective. As this programme is recorded and replayed, participants can identify their failings and improve upon them, and their success likewise can be used by others in their *da'wah* work.

b. *Computer*

The invention of the printing press in the 1450s revolutionized education in Europe at the time – knowledge, until then confined to the Church, reached a wider public. The computer is the radical invention of our times. Apart from providing numerous functions and facilities, it has accelerated the pace of development in all fields. It has given rise to a new culture, a new language and a new form of address. It is imperative for the worker of the Islamic movement to gain expertise in this new technology. The use of electronic technology as evidenced in the Gulf War and the War in Afghanistan and Iraq has made the need to master it all the more pressing.

A single computer suffices for running an office. It may compile and present information and accounts, draw up charts and other graphic aids, within a few minutes. A CD-ROM disk can hold all addresses, telephone numbers, daily engagements; indeed huge libraries can be stored. Multi-media devices provide access to sound and pictures. One can hold normal conversations through computers. The computer is thus a problem-solving device. Moreover, it is no longer a bulky object – some can be operated on the palm of a hand.

c. *Internet*

Throughout the 1990s and since the Internet has brought about a revolution in the world of communication. A computer, modem and a telephone are needed for it. The charges are equivalent to a local call. One may send a message within a few seconds. By pushing a button, which does not entail much hardship or expense, one can communicate all over the world. This explains why the Internet has replaced the telephone and fax. Millions of individuals worldwide are linked through internet services. One can also communicate with world leaders, governments, international institutions and companies with the help of the Internet. More importantly, one can contact or even hold conferences over distances with professional colleagues on subjects of his choice. Apart from international links, the Internet can be used for routine correspondence and communication within the country. If an e-mail facility is available in all branches of the movement, postal charges can be saved in that a circular can be sent at the same time to all the branches.

A scholar can access all the libraries in the world through the Internet, and may procure all sorts of information and reference material. One may scan many newspapers and magazines, without incurring any charge, and download material, also free of charge. However, this medium is also subject to abuse – to promote obscenity, for example. Also, unscrupulous persons can use it to rob banks and other companies by gaining access to confidential information. Its vulnerability to abuse for committing the worst of crimes reminds one of Mawlānā Rūmī's couplets in which he perceptively remarks that if knowledge is obtained for gratifying one's base desires, it is as dangerous as a snake. However, if it is done for the sake of self-reform, it acts as a sincere friend. The Prophet (peace and blessings be upon him) used to make the following supplication: 'O Lord! Make the knowledge which You have granted me beneficial for me. Grant me only such knowledge which is beneficial.' (Ḥākim)

4. LEADERSHIP QUALITIES

The success of the movement depends much on its leaders. Their qualities should include knowledge and piety, conscientiousness, firm conviction, undaunting resolve and consistency; also, patience, forbearance, insightful reflection, self-confidence and spirituality. These qualities inspire in others the urge to strive and sacrifice.

It is not blameworthy to develop leadership qualities for serving the cause of faith and directing fellow human beings to the straight way. It is an altogether different matter to manipulate things in a bid for power and greatness. Allah obviously disapproves it in saying that He will reserve the abode of the Hereafter only for those who do not lord it over others on the earth and do not cause any corruption (al-Qaṣaṣ 28:83). It is laudable to take the initiative in directing people to the straight way. The pious, according to the Qur'an, pray that they be appointed leader of the righteous ones (al-Furqān 25:74). While elucidating the above verse, Mawlānā Mawdūdī observes: 'This supplication is for gaining excellence in obedience to Allah and piety. They want to excel others in acts of virtue. They are not content with piety. Rather, they want to be the leaders of the pious so that virtues may flourish all over the world under their leadership.' (*Tafhīm al-Qur'ān*, vol. 3, p. 471) It is this motive that accounted for the Prophet Joseph's assuming high office in Egypt.

a. *Originality in thought and action*

The most important qualities in a leader are originality, energy, concentration and efficiency. Allah has endowed us with many abilities, but we fail to use these properly. Our thinking should stand out for its originality. For blind conformity to convention does not bring about any revolution in society. The challenges confronting the Muslim community and the internal dynamics of the movement call for serious reflection and solutions to problems. In the words of Iqbal, the glory of a community consists in its originality of thought, since that facilitates and enriches life.

Originality of thought consists in taking the initiative and being creative. Without this, problems cannot be solved. We may avoid taking any radical step for fear of making a mistake. This attitude can dissuade us from exploring new avenues. Iqbal's message on this count is loud and clear. He urges that we should find our own way, that it is a misfortune to follow blindly the way of others. If one commits a lapse in finding a new way, it will bring him some reward, though it may appear like a sin. This illustrates the *ḥadīth* which points out that a *mujtahid* is rewarded even for his mistake. We have before us the illustrious examples of the Messengers. The Qur'ān discusses at length their methodology of preaching. They found a way of presenting *da'wah* in accordance with the circumstances of their times. We should develop the ability to focus on the issues confronting us and reflect upon them with a view to fathoming all their aspects. We should be able to find a solution with the help of our expertise. Islam lays emphasis on the remembrance of Allah and other modes of worship in that these help one concentrate. This concentration is the key to good planning. A plan drawn up after serious thinking is easier to implement, because many of the problems have been foreseen. If a factory lacks skilled workers, fuel, raw material, equipment and other facilities, it is bound to suffer failures. The field of *da'wah* is much more onerous. Any negligence or forgetfulness may greatly damage the cause of the movement.

b. *Planning*

It goes without saying that the ability to plan is an essential requisite of the leader of the movement. He should set his eyes clearly on the goal and identify the stages to its attainment. After identifying the objective and fixing priorities, some progress can be made towards the realization of the stated goals.

c. *Confidence, intuition and driving force*

A leader is obliged to take his followers along with him. This requires their trust in him and commitment to surrender and sacrifice. This is possible only when the leader makes this part of their consciousness. The leader should make them understand that their sacrifice is praiseworthy, that their abilities are properly utilized, that opportunities exist for their self-development. They should have a strong feeling that their viewpoint is taken into account in arriving at a decision.

CHAPTER 4

How to Attain Self-development

Khurram Murad

THE MEANING AND OBJECTIVE OF
SELF-DEVELOPMENT

Self-development is both important and indispensable in human
life. Everyone cherishes the hope of self-development. Why should
this be so?

Its importance and desirability

We all labour in our lives in order to achieve our goals or ideals.
There is joy in attaining these goals or ideals. Let us disregard at
this juncture the nature of the goals – whether high or low,
extensive or narrow, physical or spiritual, individual or collective,
or good or evil. What is noteworthy is that special preparation is
needed for each of them.

It is a different matter whether the goals are worthy of one's attention. The noteworthy point of our purpose is that as one develops an attachment to one's goal, one becomes ardent to achieve it, to succeed.

The Qur'ān employs the words *fawz* and *falāḥ* for success. If we reflect on the meaning of these Qur'ānic expressions, we will be better able to follow the Qur'ānic passages which invite man to real success and felicity. As we are drawn towards an ideal, we invest the necessary means and resources in the effort to attain it. We improve upon and adapt our means and resources in that pursuit and waste no opportunity to gain success.

Let us make another point at this juncture. A verbal declaration in speech or writing is not the measure of our commitment to an ideal. The true measure is whether we gather the necessary means and resources to realize it and how far we devote ourselves heart and soul to this pursuit.

Another noteworthy point is that if we are clear in our minds about our goal and are attached to it, it guides us, like a lighthouse or compass. At times, we do not need to draw upon any resources; the ideal dictates what resources are needed and how they are to be employed. It identifies the landmarks, shows the way, instructs in methodology and helps us to be oriented to it.

The ideal, once again, determines the means and resources needed and their use. For example, one who aspires to be a soldier does not need to gain literary skills. Rather, he should develop military skills. Literary skills are essential for one who wants to become a writer.

However, it is essential for realizing any ideal to have the right personality. The term 'personality' is used here in its broadest sense. Included in it are one's physical and mental faculties, other abilities and potentials, heart – feelings and emotions – and character –

conduct and morals. Self-development consists in developing the personality in such a way that we are enabled to realize the ideal.

Without self-development we cannot attain our ideal. We cannot gain what we want, fully or partially, without the requisite preparation. We may acquire this preparation through a well-laid-out training programme in an organized way. But we may also acquire it without deliberate effort if it is granted to us. We gain self-development both consciously and unconsciously.

There is another kind of training which is related to the body, especially the faculties and skills, of hearing, seeing and understanding. We may train our bodies consciously. But it is significant that whether we want it or not, such training is imparted to us – this is an aspect of the omnipotence and mercy of our Lord Who arranges for such training. It commences with our birth and lasts until our death. Without this training man cannot live a proper life or even play a meaningful role.

The other development is of our inner being, of our mind and heart, of our knowledge and action, of our emotions and feelings, of our morals, in sum, of our character and conduct. Although man is granted this partly by birth, he owes it in part also to his surroundings. On the whole, however, this development very much depends on our conscious efforts. However, these efforts represent at best only a requisite. For it is Allah, our real and true Lord Who provides it. For, without His help and patronage, man cannot achieve anything. Nothing in this universe can exist on its own. Everyone is dependent upon His will and dispensation. It goes without saying that no other development is more important than this.

By the mercy of Allah, we are blessed with mental, physical, academic and professional skills, as well as the necessary competence to enable us to accomplish major tasks. This blessing gives us the potential for good conduct, unblemished character and the best morals. Of all things in the world, the most precious is excellent character and conduct. It is to be valued greatly. It endears us to others, earning their trust and affection. Nonetheless, we can gain nearness to our Lord and Paradise only by dint of sufficient effort and training. Given this, nothing could be more valuable than such effort; we should be totally committed to it, for it is the means for realizing our ideal.

The Qur'ān links one's success in both the worlds with self-purification and self-development. The Qur'ān proclaims that one who purifies himself attains success and felicity (al-A'lā 87: 14; see also al-Shams 91:9). The Qur'ān promises him the eternal gardens of Paradise and exalted rank (Ṭā Hā 20:76).

The objective of self-development – Paradise

What should be our main goal to which all our efforts for self-development should be directed? This has to be decided at the outset so that we may develop a personality fitted to our ideal and the ways and means needed for it. For example, if one who is interested in gaining knowledge will enroll himself in academic institutions, sit at the feet of scholars, devote himself to books and writings and develop the abilities to articulate his viewpoint. By the same token, if his ideal is to attain spiritual growth, he will turn to centres of spiritual retreat and monasteries, do spiritual exercises and concentrate on meditation, etc. Likewise, if he aims to succeed in warfare he must disregard academic pursuits and spiritual exercises and focus his energy on military skills.

It goes without saying that our greatest ideal should be to enter Paradise and win Allah's pleasure in the eternal life of the Hereafter. In other words, we should strive to escape Allah's wrath and hellfire. We may be saved from hellfire and His wrath and thus may be admitted to Paradise, winning His pleasure. The latter is actually more important than Paradise, as is specified in the Qur'ān (al-Tawbah 9:72). However, there is no material difference between the two. One's desire for Paradise proceeds from his seeking Allah's pleasure. If Allah is pleased with someone, He will defend him against hellfire, admit him to Paradise and bless him with His pleasure. As to those who contend that they are keen only on winning His pleasure, having nothing to do with Paradise, they are ignorant of the meaning of divine pleasure. For the Qur'ān speaks of the true believers as those who sell their selves in order to win His pleasure (al-Baqarah 2:207). At another place, the Qur'ān declares: 'Allah has purchased from the believers their lives and wealth in exchange for Paradise for them.' (al-Tawbah 9:111)

Allah has explicitly instructed us that the goal of all our worldly activities should be to secure admission to Paradise in the abiding life of the Hereafter. Man is asked to choose between the life of this world or Paradise (al-Ḥadīd 57:20). All worldly things are deceptive and illusory, and we will leave everything behind at death. All that exists on earth is mortal and ephemeral. The abiding being is only of Allah, Most Glorious and Most Noble. All glittering worldly objects are subject to decay, just as the sun and the moon set. If we take this life as our objective, all our efforts will come to naught. The Qur'ān therefore directs: 'Vie with one another in seeking the forgiveness of your Lord and towards Paradise, whose extent is equal to the heavens and the earth.' (al-Ḥadīd 57:21). At another place too the Qur'ān urges man to race towards Paradise (Āl 'Imrān 3:133). Throughout one's life one should consistently race towards Paradise, without looking aside and without pausing. In other words, self-development should be wedded to the goal of winning this race. Success brings joy and colour to life. However, the greatest success is to enter Paradise. Allah says: 'All of you will get your recompense in full on the Day of Judgement. The successful one is he who escapes hellfire and is admitted to Paradise.' (Āl 'Imrān 3:185) The Qur'ān speaks of it as a great success. At sixteen places the Qur'ān refers to one's admission to Paradise as his great success, and in more than one hundred places the bounties of Paradise are described. In some passages one particular bounty is discussed at length and man is attracted towards it. The Qur'ān asks man to make the bounties of Paradise his goal. Admission to Paradise represents the highest success imaginable and man is urged to work for it. He is repeatedly exhorted to work for this cause (al-Ṣaffāt 37:61; al-Muṭaffifīn 83:26). The bounties of Paradise are held out as a reward and man is directed to look to it as his ideal, which he will realize at the end of worldly life. 'O soul in tranquillity! Return to your Lord, well-pleased and well-pleasing! Enter then among My slaves, and enter My Paradise.' (al-Fajr 89: 27-30)

Single-minded devotion

The first step in self-development is to become devoted single-mindedly to Paradise, to resolve that it constitutes the goal of life and that all efforts should be directed to attaining it. The objective of self-development should be to become deserving of this success. It is important to determine upon this with single-minded devotion. It is a life-long decision that should come after much reflection and that needs to be rehearsed throughout life. One cannot reach this decision unless one knows the way. In the absence of focus on the goal, one will only wander and stumble, unable to reach the destination. Regrettably, most of our problems related to self-development arise from duality of behaviour on this count. We should take a plunge in the direction of seeking to enter Paradise, with total, emotional and psychological commitment. If we take the first step on this path with commitment and devotion, it will work wonders.

Before that first step, it will be useful to do the ablution, and offer two *rak'ah* of prayers with utmost concentration and devotion, recalling the punishment of hell and the bounties of Paradise and thinking of the time when the angel of death will say: 'Your time is over. Now accompany me.' We should think of the moment when we will stand before Allah and our fate will be decided. With this preparation, we should resolve to do our best to enter Paradise. We should often and fervently supplicate Allah with this prayer though the wording of the supplication is discretionary – the Prophet (peace and blessings be upon him) used to make it in these words: 'O Allah! I seek from You Paradise and protection against every word and deed that may draw me closer to hellfire.' (Ibn Mājah); 'O Allah! I seek from You such faith as can never be taken away from me, and such bounties as can never end, and such pleasure as does not exhaust and exalted rank in Paradise.' (Ibn Abī Shaybah) One should seek the Prophet's company in Paradise.

Improving one's morals and manners, one's character and conduct is a life-long activity, which may be carried out in stages. Though we may be momentarily affected by the temptations of greed and lust, we should strive to resist them, and restrain such appetites. One should, however, try to restrain his greed and lust.

Blessings and rewards

The decision to seek Paradise is necessary. For it will determine the ways and means, the methodology of the self-development we seek. That decision will serve as the criterion for choosing what to do and what to avoid, which qualities to develop and which to shun. We should decide all this in light of the question – what will draw us closer to Paradise and what will land us in hell. We need to have a very clear idea as to what pleases Allah and what angers Him. We may encounter difficulty in addressing some particular legal issues, but the commitment to enter Paradise will serve as our best teacher and guide.

It is that commitment which will inspire the effort of self-development. If a person is committed to his goal and resolves to achieve it, the commitment suffices to show him the way to appropriate self-development. The desire to seek the pleasure of Allah acts as the constant impetus and keeps one on the right track. There are historical precedents. Some persons came to Makka, embraced the faith, learnt some Qur'ānic *surahs* and returned, striking a deal regarding Paradise. These instances are best illustrated by the career of Ṭufail ibn 'Amr Dausī and Abū Dharr Ghifārī. They returned when the Prophet (peace and blessings be upon him) had arrived in Madina. Throughout, they adhered to Islam and achieved increase of faith.

Once we take the decision, we should realize that all goals other than that of admission to Paradise are not real. Self-development is not itself the goal. The same holds true for excellent conduct and unblemished character, *da'wah* and *jihād* and ascendancy of Islam and establishing faith. All of these are but means for entering Paradise. The more righteous the believer is, the more committed he will be to the Hereafter. All other goals are short-lived. If we grasp this point fully, it will help us overcome many obstacles in the way of self-development. It will help us resolve many problems and strike at the roots of many distractions, and ease the labours for self-development. We will find it easier to fulfill the obligations not only of self-development but also of faith as a whole, since the prescribed religious duties must be discharged as a part of training and self-development. Faith is the way of self-development.

If an individual wants to achieve something but is unable to do so, or if he tries to renounce something but fails to do so, or if he wants to amend his person in a particular way but is disappointed, none of this should demoralize him. For these are not the objectives in themselves. Paradise is the only objective. It is the reward for every effort. We have the opportunity to seek repentance after every sin and forgiveness is intrinsically related to Paradise. If others reject our call to truth, if they are offensive, if we do not achieve any progress in the cause of faith even after years of striving – even then we should still keep on going with determination and courage. For our goal all along is Paradise itself.

This goal will content us in that we shall not be seeking perfection. We will not leave the project incomplete (or un-attempted) on account of the imperfection in others. For perfection befits Allah alone. There are angels who cannot commit a sin, but Paradise is not their objective. Whenever the believer notes his own imperfection or failings, he should take refuge in Allah, seek His forgiveness and move in the direction of His forgiveness and Paradise.

Its all-embracing nature

We must avoid misunderstanding that taking Paradise as the goal rules out the need for self-development. Paradise is such a comprehensive goal that it takes into account every form of self-development. For example, honesty helps one enter Paradise. Likewise, being dutiful and discharging one's obligations efficiently paves the way for Paradise. If one is engaged in farming or business and fulfills the need of others, this too will contribute to one's admission to Paradise. Islam instructs that one should renounce all that is vain. Using our time properly will help one win Paradise. Likewise, offering prayers on time will also help in realizing his goal. Doing things on time and being true to one's word are virtues which make one deserving of Paradise. Indeed, fulfilling one's promise is a virtue of the highest degree for which one will be admitted to Paradise. Seen in this way, every form of self-development, not linked in any way to unlawful things is meant for entering Paradise. It is thus an all-embracing goal.

The first step: The first step to self-development is to make Paradise (and nothing else) one's goal, and to set one's eyes steadily on it. One should be concerned only with this goal and direct all efforts towards it. The decision should be deliberately taken after being firmly persuaded. Then, it needs to be engraved on the heart and mind. Then mind and tongue both continually refreshed with it.

SELF-DEVELOPMENT IS NATURAL AND MANAGEABLE

While it seems easy to have a will to enter Paradise – everyone must desire this – the self-development needed to attain Paradise seems to be a hard task. At times we may feel that it is impossible to lead life in a manner that may make us worthy of admission to Paradise; we may think it is beyond our capacity to lead such a life.

However, when we take the first step for self-development – by resolving consciously to seek Allah's pleasure and seeking Paradise as the only goal of life – we should do so in the firm conviction that self-development is natural and practicable, that it is possible for us to gain entry into Paradise, that it will be natural for us because we were meant for this way and this goal. This is a realization that we need to rehearse and refresh and reinforce all the time.

That it is natural and manageable does not mean that we will not have to experience hardship for self-development, or that we will not have to strive and struggle on this path. We will indeed have to bear with difficulties, unpleasantness, suffering and hard stages. What is implied is that we will be provided with the courage and determination needed to withstand the hardships. For everything that is demanded of man is within his capacity.

Why is it natural? Our contention is not that self-development is easy, but that it is and should be seen to be natural. Let us try to grasp this seemingly difficult statement. Its naturalness is a necessary part of its being the very objective for which man has been created. It is part of Allah's lordship, mercy and justice.

Why has Allah granted life to man on this planet earth? Obviously so as to test man whether he follows the straight way or a false path, whether he acts gratefully or ungratefully towards Allah, whether he professes belief or indulges in unbelief, whether he obeys Allah or revolts against Him, whether he worships Allah alone or takes others as gods besides Him. Whatever be the mode of its expression, the bare fact is that Allah seeks to test man: 'He it is Who created death and life in order to test you as to who among you does best.' (al-Mulk 67:2), 'We showed him the way, whether he be grateful or ungrateful.' (al-Insān 76:3)

Since his life is a test, man is granted authority and freedom. That follows necessarily. It would be pointless to test a creature compelled to act in a particular manner. It does not befit Allah's mercy and justice that He would compel man to his choice of thought or action. Since man is being tested and is promised reward or punishment as a result of the test, he is provided with the necessary freedom and authority. The sun, the moon, the stars and the angels cannot disobey Allah in the least. However, they are not held responsible either, nor are they promised the reward of Paradise.

It is a unique test

Though the period of the test is very short, its resultant reward or punishment is eternal. What is with man is short-lived whereas what is with Allah is eternal (al-Naḥl 16:96). Since the admission to Paradise is contingent upon self-development and since Paradise is the goal of life, Allah decided by His Lordship and mercy that the way to Paradise through self-development should be natural and accessible to everyone. One notes the manifestations of His Lordship and mercy in all walks of daily life. Air is essential for man's existence, we cannot survive long without it. Accordingly, it is in abundant supply everywhere, accessible to everyone and available without effort on our part. Likewise, water is essential for life, the need for it next only to air. Water too is everywhere and relatively accessible albeit not in the same easy abundance as air. In the same way, self-development, on which hinges one's success in eternal life, should also be natural and accessible to everyone, as air and water are.

Everyone is subject to testing and the goal of Paradise is placed before everyone. It would have been discordant with Allah's mercy and justice that, having subjected man to this test, having asked him to race towards it and having placed Paradise as a reward, He would have made the way to Paradise hard or inaccessible to everyone. We note that Allah has undertaken the responsibility of guiding man to the way to Paradise. Let us recall some of the relevant Qur'ānic passages: 'It is upon Us to give guidance, and unto Us belong the Hereafter and this world.' (al-Layl 92:12-13) Significantly enough, the way to Paradise, the way of obedience to Him and of faith is described as easy: 'As for him who gives in charity and keeps his duty to Allah and fears Him, and believes in good, We will make smooth for him the path of ease.' (al-Layl 92:5-7) Also, 'Allah intends for you ease, and He does not want to make things difficult for you.' (al-Baqarah 2: 185) 'Allah wishes to lighten the burden for you and man was created weak.' (al-Nisā' 4:28) In the same vein, the Prophet (peace and blessings be upon him) declared that the way of faith, of Paradise, of self-development is easy. He repeatedly directed his Companions: 'Make faith easy, not hard and difficult. Console people with glad tidings. Do not repel them by making things difficult for them.' We should therefore believe and accept the tiding that it is a necessary part of the test to which we have been put that the way of self-development, faith and Paradise is natural and manageable.

Part of Allah's mercy and justice

It runs counter to Allah's mercy and justice that on the one hand He would have invited man to the goal of Paradise, (as stated in al-Baqarah 2:221; Yūnus 10:25) and asked man to race towards it (Āl ʿImrān 3:133), and on the other that He would have made this way so difficult that no one could follow it. It does not befit His mercy that He would have put us to a test with the intention to fail us. Once, when the Prophet (peace and blessings be upon him) was asked by a woman whether a mother can hurl her baby into fire, it brought tears to his eyes and he remarked: 'No! However, people take others as god besides Him.' Allah says: 'Why should Allah punish you if you have thanked Him and have believed in Him? And Allah is Ever-Appreciative and All-Knowing.' (al-Nisā' 4:147)

112

As the believer moves on the way of self-development, he should proceed with the conviction that it is an easy, a practicable way. Allah has not put man to the test in order to fail him. He is not intent in man's failure. He will not derive any benefit from punishing man. What is demanded of man is perfectly manageable. For man has been provided with all that is needed for him to pass the test successfully.

Aspects of ease

There are many aspects of the naturalness or ease of the way of self-development. We will however, focus only on three aspects, which are essential.

1. IT IS IN ACCORDANCE WITH THE HUMAN NATURE

Since Allah has made the love for goodness and virtue innate in human beings, it is familiar to him. Man is naturally drawn towards good in that it is in line with his sensibility. Even a person of bad character is bound to appreciate such virtues as honesty, sympathy, good conduct, justice, integrity, truthfulness and being true to one's word. Everyone naturally detests murder, injustice, excess, bad manners and jealousy. It is normal to feel gratified on doing something good; it gives peace of mind. By the same token, it is normal to feel tormented on committing evil; it makes one feel debased. The Prophet (peace and blessings be upon him) described virtue and vice in these terms to his Companions. It is a part of the essential human nature with which all humans are born. Therefore, the way of virtue and goodness is both straight and easy. It tends to be hard in that we have distorted ourselves. If a twisted thing does not fit a given space, the fault is not with the space. If nothing grows on a rock, the rain is not to be blamed for it. If we adapt our heart and nature to virtues, it will be easy for us to follow this way. The Qur'ān teaches this insight that Allah has made it easy for man to follow this way (al-Layl 92:7). Likewise, it is easy to keep one's heart intact and sound. We will take up this point later.

2. LIFE AS A WHOLE IS A TRAINING GROUND

Another aspect is that Allah has made the whole of life and the whole universe our training ground. Obviously some duties have been prescribed such as prayers, *zakāh* and *ḥajj*. However, every incident, every experience, every mental condition, every bounty, every suffering, every calamity, every virtue, every evil and every encounter with other creatures in this universe has many lessons for man, provided one is willing to learn.

As to those who constantly draw these lessons, Allah describes them as those who remember Him, standing, sitting and reclining (Āl 'Imrān 3:191). It is promised that divine signs will be shown to them in the universe (Fuṣṣilat 41:53).

Those who are devoted to the book of Revelation, and the book of nature and life, and who are always drawing lessons from them do not stand in need of any special training course, although such courses can be helpful. However these can be really effective if they help man appreciate the whole of life as a training ground. With a little reflection we realize that every good deed we do is a means for self-development. We should regard it as a virtue, cherish it and thank Allah for having enabled us to do it, look forward to its reward and derive contentment from that. We should seek divine light by doing good deeds. We should remember that virtue is an inclusive concept in the Islamic tradition – earning a livelihood and spending on oneself and one's family, doing business, planting trees and eating of their fruits and offering them to birds and animals – all these constitute virtue. Even if the fruits are taken by birds and animals or simply stolen, it will be credited to one's account as a good deed. Marital relations too constitute a good deed. Every good deed is a blessing for the doer.

Though committing sin is a major cause of despair, this too can be turned to good account. As the person realizes that he has committed a sin, he should weep and his heart should fill with sorrow and remorse. He should firmly believe that Allah alone can save him against its dire consequences. This should prompt him to turn wholly to Allah and weep. The whole sequence is immensely helpful in the process of self-development. I am not suggesting that one should commit sins. It is of course, essential to abhor and avoid sins. However, it is part of divine dispensation that man cannot escape from committing a sin. If he is drawn towards a sin and yet restrains himself out of fear of Allah, this constitutes a good deed. The more serious the sin the greater the virtue of controlling oneself. Allah says: 'But as for him who feared standing before his Lord, and restrained himself from impure desires and lust, Paradise will be his abode.' (al-Nāzi'āt 79:40-41)

The same holds true for divine bounties. Every divine favour is a means for man's testing and self-development. It holds true for every bounty in general, be it breathing, a morsel of food, a sip of water, defending the body, and all sustenance. The same applies to divine gifts that are special to particular individuals. These should remind us of Allah Who has conferred these bounties, and our hearts should overflow with gratitude to Him. We should not attribute our expertise or skills to our own knowledge, nor ascribe them to others as being their gift. Rather, we should sincerely thank Allah, acknowledging Him as the true source of all good. This attitude serves as a remedy for moral and spiritual ailments. The more one thanks Allah, the more generously one is rewarded by Him. If someone thanks Allah for having enabled him to do good, it will help him to do more good acts, in turn enhancing his self-development.

The same is true for every suffering and calamity that may afflict a person. These too serve as means for self-development. We should recognize that all events are caused by Him without Whose leave even a leaf cannot move. Furthermore, He is Most Compassionate, Most Merciful and is caring and well-wishing to mankind. We must bear up in the face of loss and suffering. Perseverance is the master key to self-development. In the absence of calamities one cannot receive the supreme felicity of Allah's mercy.

3. It is practicable

It does not befit Allah's mercy and justice that He would ask man to do something beyond his capacity or put man to a test that he cannot undergo. It runs counter to the fundamentals of justice. How can someone be tested in something of which he is ignorant or incapable, and then punished for failure? Having expressed this fundamental principle, the Qur'ān draws attention to the following dispensation of Allah – it comes in the concluding part of *Sūrah al-Baqarah* (2:286), which gives expression to many broad principles of faith – Allah does not burden a soul beyond its capacity; every soul is rewarded for that good that it has earned, and is punished for the evil that it has earned. The essential principle is stated at several places in the Qur'ān. If someone is made to utter a blasphemous statement, although he is firmly persuaded of faith, he will not be taken to task or reckoned a sinner for what he said or did under compulsion having no choice in the matter. Also, the failings that arise out of forgetfulness are pardoned by Allah. And thoughts that cross one's mind involuntarily and the temptations to sin are also not punishable. For man is too helpless with regard to these. On the contrary, if he is drawn towards a sin yet checks himself, he is given the glad tidings of divine reward. There is no accountability for the ever-changing state of the heart. As Islam spread, the obligation to keep night vigil was withdrawn. Since Allah knew that it would not be possible for all Muslims to discharge this duty, He pardoned them and directed that as much of the Qur'ān be recited as is possible.

Allah directs that one should fear Allah as He is to be feared (Āl 'Imrān 3:102). On hearing this verse the Companions trembled in nervousness and fear. For it is beyond man's capacity to fear Allah in the due measure. It was then clarified that the believer should fear Him as much as it is possible for him to do. Fearing Allah is another means of self-development. We can therefore safely infer that we should seek self-development to the limit of our capacity. We are not asked to do anything beyond our capacity. Whenever the Prophet (peace and blessings be upon him) took the oath of allegiance regarding obedience and *jihād*, he qualified the statement with 'to the extent possible'.

It is perfectly within one's capacity to discharge the duties prescribed by Allah or to refrain from what is forbidden by Him. It is not beyond man's power to observe the limits set by Him, whether these be related to acts of worship, *jihād*, eating and drinking, spending, morals, mutual dealings, keeping one's word, justice, doing good, maintaining the ties of kinship, or negative qualities like jealousy, spying, backbiting and thinking ill of others. If one is unable to follow these commands, or if one resorts to some pretext to evade them, no ruling by a jurist consult will avail. We cannot escape divine reckoning by offering an excuse to fellow human beings. The individual would do better to think whether he would be able to convince Allah with his false pretext – when Allah knows the manifest and the hidden. If he has a genuine ground for his inability, Allah will accept it. He will not be taken to task for a failing that he cannot help. Nor will it reflect poorly on his self-development. However, if it is unacceptable to Allah, no ruling will help him. Nor will others carry his burden. This line of thinking should facilitate for him the course of his self-development.

The believer should therefore, proceed on the way of self-development with a conviction that there is nothing that can prevent him from the way to Paradise, and nothing that can deter him from this way because it cannot be beyond his capacity. This conviction will help him overcome many difficulties in the way, and settle many of the doubts and complaints often made by those struggling for self-purification.

Voluntary and involuntary acts

The deciding factor is whether something is voluntary or involuntary. Some people claim often that they cannot control this or that habit or perform this or that duty or they cannot renounce some unlawful practice. Let them study closely whether it really is absolutely beyond their capacity. If Allah has asked man to do something, it must certainly be within man's power to do it. As already indicated, Allah does not demand anything of man which is beyond his capacity. One should not be unduly concerned about matters about which there are no divine commands, nor should these distract one from doing good.

Obstacles and misapprehensions

Despair is the biggest obstacle in the way of self-development, and its effect on the quality of effort. Man is vulnerable to all sorts of thoughts that cross his mind, including those about Allah and His Messengers and their teachings. At times, one is strongly drawn towards sin, and overwhelmed by loss of hope. However, man is not answerable for the thoughts crossing his mind; he can not prevent this happening. Such thoughts do not by themselves bar one from entering Paradise, and therefore one should not feel demoralized. Our obligation is only to strive to stop evil thoughts crossing our minds and instead, develop pious ideas. We should be content with this effort. However, in spite of determined intent, we are apt to weaken in our resolve. It is beyond man to have an unchallenged resolve. Allah puts man to test continually in order to ascertain the firmness of his resolve. Failure in resolve will not by itself be punished nor entail divine wrath.

The difficulty is the sinning related to weakness of resolve. An individual may commit sin and do so repeatedly, notwithstanding repeated repentance. He may commit evil knowingly, in spite of his understanding of relevant divine commands. Human nature is only too susceptible to give in to the base desires of the self. Yet this should not make one despondent. It is not within man's power not to commit any sin at all or to avoid the repetition of sin despite repentance. Only the angels and Messengers are immune against sinning. Man has been granted freedom of choice and this inevitably provides him with a chance to commit sin. However, the same freedom may be exercised to gaining entry into Paradise. Allah makes it a point to link His forgiveness with admission to Paradise.

As the person's mind is troubled by evil thoughts, he suffers from despondency. Likewise, if he is unable to rise to the required standard, he is filled with despair. He is tormented by the fluctuations in his spiritual state. He must, nonetheless, realize that he does not have any control over the conditions of his thought. He is answerable only for his actions. Love and fear for Allah and total devotion to Him are, no doubt, ideals and he should draw upon every conceivable means to attain them. However, he will not be taken to task for the quantum or degree of his feelings and aspirations. On the basis of these, he will not be denied Paradise. Therefore, he should not permit himself to collapse into despair and despondency. Everyone looks for perfection even though it is not attainable. Indeed, perfection runs counter to being human, and so it is vain to pursue the unattainable. One can also be disappointed on observing lapses and weaknesses in others and give up on one's own self-development. This response is the height of foolishness. One is not empowered to achieve self-development for others. No one can carry another's burden in this respect. One should rather, be concerned with one's own conduct and consistently follow the straight way while working for reform of oneself and of others.

Points to remember

Let us realize clearly that we should take Paradise as our goal and resolve to attain self-development. The first and foremost point is that the way of self-development, of faith and guidance, and of Paradise, is practicable and natural. Only if we regard it as something unnaturally arduous, does it appear difficult. Therefore, the above points should be always brought to mind; doing so sustains and improves morale. As we work with confidence we will not suffer from loss of hope. Allah is always there to help and support us.

ﻬﻬﻬﻬ

INTENTION AND ACTION ARE ESSENTIAL

Self-development is necessary to gain success in both the worlds. One cannot enter Paradise without undergoing self-purification and self-development. Self-development is indeed the natural way to gain entry into Paradise, and perfectly practicable. However, we must be mindful that we are fully responsible for our self-development. We should resolve to do what we intend and do everything in this regard. Without this there cannot be any self-development.

The first and foremost condition is one's intention and action. Allah looks for these and He has promised reward for them. There is no substitute for lack of intention, and if one fails to supply this, it cannot be compensated in any way. Nothing can replace one's intention and action. No one can do this work on another's behalf. For every individual is obliged in his personal capacity to attain self-development. If he does not practise what he learns or is not prepared to learn anything, no training can help him. His faith and good action alone can win Allah's forgiveness and mercy which will, in turn, admit him to Paradise. This constitutes the fundamental principle of self-development. It is self-evident and clear. Notwithstanding its manifest nature, it is regrettably ignored. It is clouded by wishful thinking and false pretexts. While disregarding this fundamental principle, one looks for false supports, which are illusory.

Law of retribution

On reflection one realizes that the fundamental principle related to self-development is in line with the purpose of our creation. It is the essence of the test to which we are put. Indeed, it is its essential precondition. We have been put to the test to see whether we do good deeds. We are therefore fully responsible for our actions.

As a matter of fact, man enjoys total authority over only his own action. This facilitates greatly the work of self-development.

For it is within our power to take any action. However, by the same token, we will be rewarded only on the basis of what we do. We entitle ourselves to Allah's mercy and forgiveness and entry into Paradise by dint of only our actions. Had we not been granted this authority over our actions, the test to which we are put would be devoid of meaning. As it is, no other can offer prayers on our behalf; no other can fast for us. Likewise, we cannot fulfill promises or serve fellow human beings, or strive for good on someone else's behalf. We cannot deserve reward or punishment for an action not performed by us. If someone compels us into committing a sin, while we are not inclined towards it, we will not face any punishment on this count. This applies even to uttering blasphemy under coercion, if one is firmly persuaded of faith. By the same token, if someone compels us into doing good, we are not entitled to any reward for it. No one can undergo self-development in our place in that it is our own obligation. If we do not make any effort for self-development, someone else's teachings cannot benefit us. Any effort for self-development from without may be likened to raining upon rocks. Needless to add, every river draws upon rainfall in proportion to its capacity while rainfall usually washes away from rocks. Allah lays down this fundamental principle thus: 'Man is rewarded for that good which he has earned, and he is punished for the evil which he has earned.' (al-Baqarah 2:286) This fundamental principle is elaborated elsewhere in the Qur'ān, with the affirmation that this eternal principle features in all the Scriptures: 'Or is he not informed of what is in the Scripture of Mūsā, and of Ibrāhīm, who fulfilled all that Allah ordered him to do: that no person burdened shall bear the burden of another. And that man can have nothing but what he does, good or bad. And that his deeds will be seen. Then he will be recompensed with a full and best recompense.' (al-Najm 53:36-41) Admission to Paradise is accordingly contingent upon one's success in the test and one's effort and striving. It leaves no doubt whatever that there may be a way other than that of action for winning Paradise; there is not.

The Qur'ān repeatedly affirms that Paradise is the reward for one's actions, especially of the pious ones. It is for those who embrace faith and do good deeds. Man is exhorted to race towards Paradise. It should be the driving force and everyone should try to excel others. This message permeates the Qur'ān. One thus realizes that wishful thinking, attending lectures, joining the company of the righteous, or the favour done by any spiritual authority cannot take one to Paradise. Without one's own intention and action to that end, one cannot enter Paradise.

Nothing else will serve the purpose

It is an error to think that one can attain self-development without any effort or action. Mere study of books, or joining of study circles cannot substitute for one's own effort, nor can listening to moving speeches or participating in a training programme. The same holds for the ministrations of some spiritual master – his favours cannot rescue one unless one is committed and takes appropriate actions. The spiritual master cannot get anything for another than himself. Were Paradise attainable without one's own intention and action, the entire argument of test and trial would be meaningless. If the individual does not make up his own mind or take any action for his self-development, then even the Prophet's company and teachings cannot bring success for him. He will still persist in error if he himself does not want to change. The Messengers were not granted such authority over others. The Qur'ān makes it plain: 'O Messenger! You cannot guide him whom you like.' (al-Qaṣaṣ 28:56) The Prophet (peace and blessings be upon him) was not granted any such authority. Nor was he entrusted with the job of forcing people, without their consent, to the way of guidance. People tainted with unbelief and hypocrisy joined the Prophet's sittings and left with the same impurities: 'They visit with unbelief and returned in the same condition.' (al-Mā'idah 5:61)

Satan's authority

If one is not inclined towards evil, Satan cannot force him to commit evil. Let us accept that Satan constantly accompanies man; he is so to speak, in man's bloodstream. He lies in ambush for man in unexpected places, constantly on the prowl. Yet he cannot compel man into doing evil. He is not granted any such authority. He cannot supersede man's authority over his action. Rather, on the Day of Judgement, he will declare: 'I had no authority over you except that I called you and you responded to me. So blame me not, but blame yourselves.' (Ibrāhīm 14:22).

Allah's help and support

Man cannot do anything without Allah's help and support. However, we must understand that divine help can rescue man only when he displays commitment and does good deeds, on his

125

way to Paradise. The Qur'ān declares this truth unequivocally, as is evident from the following passages: 'Allah guides to Himself whoever turns to Him.' (al-Shūrā 42:13). 'And whoever repents and does good deeds; then verily, he repents towards Allah with true repentance.' (al-Furqān 25:71); 'And verily I am indeed forgiving to him who repents, believes and does good deeds, and then remains constant in doing them.' (Ṭā Hā 20:82); 'Remember Me, I will remember you.' (al-Baqarah 2:152); 'Fulfill your covenant with Me, I will fulfill My covenant with you.' (al-Baqarah 2:40); 'If you are grateful, I will grant you more.' (Ibrāhīm 14:7)

If the person has the commitment and good deeds to his credit, he is promised glad tidings. The Prophet (peace and blessings be upon him) pointed out that as one performs his obligations, it pleases Allah. When he does such deeds which are not obligatory yet are pleasing to Him, his sight, hearing and limbs act in accordance with Allah's will. Man is obliged to perform his religious duties. If he fails to do so, he cannot get what he is promised.

In another *ḥadīth* he says: 'Whoever approaches Allah a little, He advances towards him. Whoever walks to Allah, He hastens towards him.' (Muslim) This indicates Allah's immense mercy for man's self-development and guiding him to Paradise. Nonetheless, His mercy is reserved for him who approaches Him and takes some steps in this direction. As to him who is indifferent and careless, and fails to take any action, he cannot obviously draw upon His abundant mercy. The condition is that one should have the commitment and make the effort. Allah has promised to give generously.

Intention suffices

Let the misunderstanding be removed altogether that one can attain anything without intention and action. Let it also be realized that Allah does not look for perfection in man's actions. Man is not obliged to gain success in his efforts. For man does not exercise any such authority. He is expected only to strive to the extent it is possible for him. All reward is promised for his striving: 'And whoever desires the Hereafter and strives for it, with the necessary efforts due for it, while he is a believer, then such are the ones whose striving shall be favoured.' (al-Isrā' 17:19)

Contained in the above passage are many Qur'ānic teachings. It strikes at the root of the obstructions in the way of self-development. For a person is, at times, overcome by despondency that his efforts will not be accepted by Allah or that he falls too far short of the expected standards. At other times, he feels that his action is devoid of the requisite state of the heart. His prayer lacks concentration and attention; he does not cry while praying. Sometimes he is distraught over the absence of the desired results. Notwithstanding his offering prayers, he cannot give up obscene and forbidden things. He fasts yet is unable to attain piety. He is full of despair over his inability to attain success. Despite his best efforts for making the call, striving and sacrifices in the cause, his call is not welcomed by people. Faith is no longer ascendant and the Islamic state is not in place. He is demoralized further by weaknesses in his resolve. Notwithstanding all efforts for self-control he is filled with despair and despondency. However, we must remember well that none of the failings and imperfections mentioned is a necessary condition for one's exclusion from Paradise. This realization can help one overcome despair, and save him from such despondency that he may give up his resolve and effort for self-development.

Intention

We have spoken frequently of intention in this context. It features also in the Qur'ān. One has full control over one's intention. It is one of the prerequisites for self-development, and is its basic ground and strength. However, we must make it clear that intention is not to be confused with wishing. This is a very common misperception. People are found saying: 'I do want to get up at *Fajr* time to offer the prayers but I just cannot get up.' This wishing to get up is not synonymous with the intention to get up. Think if one has to catch a plane in the early hours or has an important appointment that promises one some good – one is sure to get up early. One will make every effort to get up in time. This is an illustration of how we execute our intention for an ordinary commitment. The same care and attention should be exercised in regard to all the requisites of faith and self-development.

One's intention takes into account the value and importance of what is sought. One's level of devotion to that thing is also a deciding factor. Therefore it is a conscious step, reflecting one's resolve. In verse 20 of *al-Shūrā* the Qur'ān employs the term 'intention' in this sense, when it speaks of someone's intention for seeking Allah's pleasure or reward in the Hereafter.

The person may weaken in his intention. His resolve may be broken altogether; or he may work contrary to what he originally intended, or just forget. Nevertheless, on the whole, the first step in the pursuit of Allah's pleasure, the Hereafter, Paradise and self-development, is one's intention. It is needed for everything that one needs to do in the cause of faith and self-development. After regret for any failure and conscious return, the intention may be instantly taken up again. In the absence of intention even a major, sustained effort to train oneself may not be fruitful. Conversely, if one has the intention, a little guidance may yield rich dividends. Even if there is no proper training, sermon, exhortation and study, intention by itself serves as a most effective teacher and guardian. For it guides one to the straight way, helps one pursue it steadily and dissuades one from taking a false path.

Single-minded devotion is needed for intention. We cannot serve God and Mammon at the same time. We cannot set our eyes on both the worlds simultaneously. One who sails on two boats can never reach his destination. A weak intention will result only in failure and demoralization. We may gain firmness of intention, if we are persuaded of the immense value of the objective – Allah, Paradise – and self-development as the means for it. The more committed we are to this goal, the firmer our intention will be. Obviously, our commitment will be strong in proportion to our devotion to Allah and Paradise. It is therefore repeatedly emphasized that we should love Allah and His Messenger and struggle in His cause more than any other thing. This explains also the vivid portrayal of the bounties of Paradise in the Qur'ān. They are projected as a living reality in order to inspire us.

Let us reiterate the point that the development and growth of one's deeds and character can be attained only gradually. It is a time-consuming process. One can instantly make up one's mind to do it. However, by the same token, one can break one's intention in no time as well. This should not, however, be an excuse to become demoralized. For one can easily and instantly resume one's intention.

Striving

If the individual has the intention, it inevitably results in his taking some action. If he cannot achieve much, he should, at least, show his readiness to move forward, his keen desire and his turning his attention to his goal. Even if he seems unable to proceed further, he should, at least, have a keen desire to do so. His eyes should be firmly fixed on the goal and he should be fired by the intense desire to approach his goal. And whenever it is possible and feasible, he should take practical steps and move forward. The Qur'ān provides a graphic picture of man's striving in the following passages: 'I have turned my face towards Him, Who has created the heavens and the earth.' (al-An'ām 6:79); 'My Prayer, my sacrifice, my living, and my dying are for Allah, the Lord of the worlds.' (al-An'ām 6:162); 'When his Lord said to him, "Submit", he said, "I have submitted myself to the Lord of the universe".' (al-Baqarah 2:131); 'Hasten earnestly to the remembrance of Allah and leave off business.' (al-Jumu'ah 62:9)

Remember that one's efforts greatly facilitate the attainment of the goal. A spiritual figure told someone in a dream to put into his mouth whatever he sees first on waking up. As the man set out, the first thing he saw was a mountain. He gave up, thinking that a mountain could not be put into the mouth. The spiritual figure appeared again and asked him to proceed nonetheless. The man climbed the mountain and at the top he came across a piece of a sweet, and put that in his mouth. Everything that we regard as demanding and strenuous regarding religious duties and the requisites of self-development, may be likened to the mountain in this parable.

The same lesson may be drawn from the incident recounted by the Prophet (peace and blessings be upon him) about someone who had killed ninety-nine people. He approached a pious person to ask him whether there was a way to repent. The pious person declared that there was no way whatever. In a fit of anger the man killed that pious person as well. Then he approached a scholar and put the same question to him. The scholar affirmed that the man could still repent, but told him that he should leave that town and move to another town inhabited by pious persons. The man duly repented and started moving towards the other town. He died on the way. This led to an argument between the angels of mercy and punishment, both of whom claimed him. The matter was resolved by another angel, who suggested that the distance be measured to determine whether he was closer to the town of pious people, in which case the angel of mercy could take him, or the opposite, in which case the angel of punishment had his claim on him. He was found to have been closer to the town of the pious people, and was accordingly taken by the angel of mercy. A whole volume could be written on the lessons implicit in this story. Yet its message is loud and clear: if one's intention is sincere and strong and he makes the effort to do something, he is helped by Allah's mercy, enabling him to reach his destination.

Final word: We must make it plain that self-development is possible only through one's intention and effort. If we have the commitment, every piece of training will prove fruitful, as we will be reinforced by Allah's mercy. But if an individual does not provide for his self-development, no one can provide it for him. We should therefore resolve to proceed further on the way. Sincere resolve constitutes the first and also the last step.

CHAPTER 5

Self-development in the Context of Man's Relationship with Allah

Amīn Aḥsan Iṣlāḥī

ĪMĀN AND ISLAM

Man's relationship with Allah is to be defined in terms of the key concepts of *īmān* and Islam. The above two terms are used interchangeably because in fact they are interdependent. Nonetheless, they are in essence the same. True *īmān* consists in embracing Islam. By the same token, Islam calls for true faith. Without faith one's claim to Islam betrays hypocrisy. This baseless claim devoid of substance will be altogether dismissed. Likewise, one's claim to *īmān*, if it is not supported by his acceptance of Islam, is absolutely false and is not accepted by *Sharī'ah*.

Īmān and Islam are intertwined

Notwithstanding the closeness between the two, there is an important difference between *Īmān* and Islam. *Īmān* is related to basic beliefs and their affirmation which serve as the foundation of a religion. Islam stands for the acts of worship and the commands and laws – obedience to which is part of *Īmān* prescribed by Allah and His Messenger. In other words, it may be held that faith is related to beliefs whereas Islam signifies one's belief. Yet this distinction is rather academic as a true believer's life reflects a perfect combination of the two. One cannot exist in isolation from the other. Neglect of either will result in the absence of both.

A common misconception

One of the most common misconceptions of our times is the assumption that one's affirmation of certain beliefs suffices for deliverance. It is done at the expense of neglecting and disregarding good deeds and morals. This misconception was initially restricted to certain sects. However, it has now crept into the whole body of believers so that it is hard to condemn it. Notwithstanding its popularity, we must affirm that this misconception runs counter to the teachings of the Qur'ān and the Prophet's *Sunnah*. In almost every instance of exhorting man to believe, the Qur'ān asks at the same time that he should do good deeds. It is therefore evident that both are intertwined. It is expected of every believer to do good deeds. For example, 'The believers are only those whose hearts quake with awe when Allah is mentioned, and when His revelations are rehearsed to them, it increases their faith and they put their trust in their Lord, who establish prayer and who spend of what We have provided them. These are they who are the true believers.' (al-Anfāl 8:2-4)

The Qur'ān likens *Īmān* to a fruit-bearing tree with its roots deeply embedded and branches spreading out, and bearing fruit in all seasons: 'Do you not see how Allah sets forth a parable? – a good word like a good tree, its roots firmly fixed, and its branches reaching the heavens: giving its fruit at every season by the command of its Lord.' (Ibrāhīm: 14:24-25)

The 'good tree' in the above passage obviously stands for *Īmān*. Its roots being deeply embedded, it signifies the faith penetrating deeply in the human nature. In other words, it is not something superficial without roots, or something that may be uprooted easily. In sharp contrast to it is unbelief which does not have any firm basis (Ibrāhīm 14:26). Faith is like a strong tree which is not brought down by storms. Moreover, it yields fruit in all seasons. Its outspread branches provide shade and refuge to everyone. The allusion here is to the blessings accruing from the pious life of a believer. Those in contact with him also derive many benefits from him. These benefits are manifest in practical life and bear out his faith. It helps the believer to attain exaltation and elevation, as is declared by Allah: 'To Him mount up goodly words and the righteous work exalts it.' (Fāṭir 35:10) We learn from this verse that goodly words ascend – it is their nature – but they need support which is provided by good deeds. Taken in this sense, it may be compared to a vine that blooms as it gains some support – without support it cannot grow well, if at all.

Going by the above analogy it may be held that true faith is contingent upon total obedience to the Prophet (peace and

135

blessings be upon him). One's conduct should provide abundant evidence for one's faith. If one's claim to faith is not substantiated by his emulation of the Prophet's model, he does not possess faith. It goes without saying that one who cannot prove his faith by this evidence cannot be taken as a believer. The Qur'ān points out: 'But no, by your Lord, they shall not really believe until they have made you (the Prophet) the judge of what is disputed among them and then find no demur in their hearts against what you have decreed and they submit with full submission.' (al-Nisā' 4:65)

The verse just quoted is addressed to the hypocrites who made a show of embracing Islam, as they were overawed by its fast-growing strength. However, they maintained close ties with the Jews in and around Madina and still enjoyed some limited political power, as the Islamic state had not yet been fully established. These hypocrites therefore moved their cases to Jewish courts rather than to the Prophet (peace and blessings be upon him), in the hope that by resorting to bribery and other unfair means they would be able to influence the court and secure judgement in their favour. The Qur'ān declares regarding these hypocrites that this practice of theirs is contrary to their claim to faith. For faith demands that they take the Prophet (peace and blessings be upon him) as the supreme ruler and abide by his decision. If they fail to do so, their claim to faith cannot be accepted. The Qur'ān brings home this point elsewhere thus: 'The faithful are those only who have faith in Allah and His Messenger and have not doubted thereafter, and have striven hard with their riches and their lives in the cause of Allah. Those, they are the truthful.' (al-Ḥujurāt 49:15)

Īmān and Islam are not static

It must be borne in mind regarding faith and Islam that these are not static entities. Rather, these are susceptible to change, and they can increase provided one takes the necessary steps. Conversely, if one does not take proper care of faith, it is liable to wither and degenerate. The law of nature applicable to all living entities holds true for faith in an equal measure. True believers achieve increase in their faith by reflecting on the objects of nature and perceive in them the glory, creative power, wisdom, mercy and Lordship of their Creator. They study with insight the laws of nature operating in the universe. (It goes without saying that the laws of nature are constant, unalterable and impartial.) Taking their cue from this insight, the believers follow strictly the commands of their Lord in every department of life and as a result are blessed with His mercy and favours. They experience a renewed vigour and zest for faith as they undergo tests and trials and withstand these, reinforced by perseverance and gratitude. Those attain growth in faith to the highest degree who reflect constantly on the Book of Allah and earnestly supplicate: 'O Lord! I invoke You by every name befitting You, which You have used of Yourself or which You have revealed in Your Book, or which You have taught to any of Your creatures, that You make the Qur'ān the spring of my heart, the light of my chest, the cure for my ailments and the remedy for my anxieties and worries.' (Aḥmad)

In the light of that long supplication, there is hardly any need to mention those who are devoid of these truths. Those who do not take any step to maintain and strengthen their faith in the above manner are liable to lose their faith altogether.

One is reminded here of the analogy of a wild plant grown in a backyard. Since it is not looked after properly, it is soon destroyed by adverse circumstances.

Allah's law regarding faith is that He, no doubt, grants faith to many. However, He enables only a few to make it grow in that they value their faith and fulfill all its obligations. His truth is stated in the Qur'ān thus: 'And recall when your Lord proclaimed: If you are grateful, I will add more (favours) unto you.' (Ibrāhīm 14:7)

One's appreciation for a Divine bounty is reflected best by one's valuing it dearly and discharging its obligations. If one fails to do so, not only can one not derive its benefits, but also suffers loss of the bounty. This is substantiated by a saying of the Prophet Jesus.

It also emerges from the Qur'ān that those believers are granted growth in their faith who consistently adhere to their faith even in the face of severe trials and sufferings. In accordance with Allah's law, they are subjected to these tests in order to prove their mettle. Allah does not let the claimants to faith go unscathed. They are tested in a variety of ways in order to ascertain whether they are sincere in their claim to faith. If they fail the test, their names are struck off the rolls of true believers. On the contrary, if they withstand all trials heroically, they are reinforced with stronger, firmer faith. This point appears in the Qur'ān: 'Do people think that they shall be left alone because they say: "We believe" and that they shall not be tested.' (al-'Ankabūt 29:2)

Allah helps and supports those who stand up to testing, as mentioned in this verse: 'They were youths who believed in their Lord and We increased them in guidance.' (al-Kahf 18:13)

Let it be pointed out that the above verse occurs in *Sūrah al-Kahf* at the juncture when they were served with a dire warning by their own community members that they would be stoned, if they did not give up their call to monotheism. Undaunted, they – far from abandoning their faith – resolved to adhere to their faith at any cost and earnestly petition Allah to grant them success in all subsequent phases. As a reward for their resolve and their fervent plea, Allah increased them so much in their faith that they were able to withstand all trials successfully and were blessed with His mercy and grace.

The Companions grew in faith even as the hypocrites tried to demoralize them by telling them that huge armies of the enemies of Islam were on their way to destroy them. Far from feeling overawed, their faith was renewed by such threats. The Qur'ān refers to the occasion: 'They tell them: "A great army is gathering against you, so fear them." However, it increased them (Muslims) in faith.' (Āl 'Imrān 3:173)

At several places the Qur'ān mentions it as an outstanding feature of true believers that when they are obstructed by their enemies, they feel rejuvenated by their faith. As to the obstacles erected in their way, the believers behave thus: 'As for the faithful, it increases them in faith and they rejoice.' (al-Tawbah 9:124) What demoralizes and enervates the hypocrites brings about an increase in the faith of true believers. This point comes out sharply in the Qur'ān: 'Allah and His Messenger have spoken the truth. Among the faithful, it only increases them in belief and self-surrender.' (al-Aḥzāb 33:22)

A caution

It is reported of Imām Abū Ḥanīfah that he did not subscribe to
the view that one's faith was subject to any increase or decrease.
This stance evidently runs counter to what we have said above. It
is likely, however, that the Imām made the above observation in
a particular context, which has since disappeared from the
discussion. Otherwise, such a distinguished Islamic scholar as
the Imām could not hold a view not supported by the Qur'ān
and the *Ḥadīth*.

It must be conceded that the Imām's observation holds true
in a narrow legal sense. As it is, in law one goes by the appearance.
It lies outside the purview of law to deal with the nature and
quality of something. In law one who affirms certain articles of
faith and performs the prescribed rituals is to be accepted as a
Muslim. A jurist cannot ascertain whether a claimant to faith
believes sincerely or merely professes his faith outwardly. Likewise,
he cannot pass any judgement on the intention and motive behind
his performance of religious rituals. There is no measure to
determine one's sincerity or hypocrisy on this count. Questions
about the nature and quality of one's faith are not a jurist's concern,
and he cannot pass judgement upon them. A jurist may, at most,
prescribe a certain standard for the citizens of an Islamic state or
that their disputes be settled with reference to it. Obviously this
standard will be universal, applicable to everyone in an equal
measure and will be decided on the basis of what one verbally
professes. As to the inner condition and the degree of
commitment, these cannot be taken as the deciding factor.

On studying the issue in this perspective, we realize that the
Imām must have expressed that view in a particular context and

in so doing he did not take a position at variance with that of the Qur'ān and the *Ḥadīth*. Nor is our stance divergent from his. Quoting the Imām's view out of its proper context makes his position appear discordant with that of the Qur'ān and the *Sunnah*. However, in its proper context, the view is entirely valid and in line with the Qur'ān and the *Sunnah*.

Islamic role models

The Qur'ān adduces the Prophets Abraham and Ishmael (peace and blessings be upon them) as perfect Islamic role models. They embodied perfect faith. We have already indicated in the introductory part of this work that *īmān* and Islam are intertwined. In essence there is no difference or distinction between the two.

The Prophet Abraham (peace and blessings be upon him) is presented as a perfect role model in view of his excellent performance in the tests related to his faith. He alone holds the distinction of being put to such a hard test and Allah Himself testifies that he secured total success in it.

Islam is generally defined as one's total surrender and obedience to Allah. A Muslim is ever ready to lay down all that he has at the command of his Lord. For a Muslim's creed is: 'Surely my prayer and my rites and my life and my death are all for Allah, Lord of the worlds.' (al-An'ām 6:162) By their excellent deeds, the Prophets Abraham and Ishmael (peace and blessings be upon them) illustrated their total surrender to Allah's will and are therefore referred to as perfect Islamic role models. They prayed that their progeny be blessed with perfect faith: 'Our Lord!

Make us submissive to You, and of our progeny a community submissive to You.' (al-Baqarah 2:128) Allah accepted their supplication and the Prophet Muḥammad (peace and blessings be upon him) represents that progeny. He organized a great community, which was called Muslim, in line with the meaning of the Prophet Abraham's petition. The Qur'ān is explicit that Allah has named the believers 'Muslims' and this name features in the Qur'ān (al-Ḥajj 22:78). It should also be borne in mind that Islam stands out as the original faith prescribed by Allah. The Qur'ān declares: 'In the sight of Allah, Islam is the *Dīn*.' (Āl 'Imrān 3:19) The Prophet Abraham (peace and blessings be upon him) professed and practised Islam. Calling Islam and Muslims by any other name is mere innovation. The Muslim community has been raised in order to uphold the message of Islam. May Allah show us the truth as it is and enable us to adhere to it, and show us falsehood as it is and enable us to shun it.

MAN'S RELATIONSHIP WITH ALLAH AND ITS BASIS

Of all the ties of man, his relationship with his Lord is obviously the first and foremost. It determines his other relationships – with fellow human beings, family, tribe, community and state. It prescribes the whole range of man's relationships with all that exists in the universe. If man gains a proper understanding of his sound relationship with Allah, severs his false ties and maintains the prescribed relationship, he will grow into an obedient servant of his Lord, a valuable member of his family, a sincere citizen of his state and a loving and caring human being concerned with the welfare of all mankind. It transforms him into a morally trained and pious person. This transformation lies at the heart of the self-development recommended by the Messengers of Allah. Conversely, if man fails to maintain any of these ties, blessings do not accrue to him and crookedness mars his conduct. We should understand from the outset that all these relationships are inter-connected; any negative quality in any of them has a bearing on our overall conduct.

On studying the Qur'ān one learns that we can establish a correct and sound relationship with Allah only if we adapt ourselves to divine attributes. Each and every divine attribute makes certain demands on our heart, our soul and our deeds. If we fulfill these demands, it signifies the forging of a perfect relationship with our Lord. These demands are clearly spelled out by the *Sharī'ah*. It is noteworthy that as the Qur'ān lays down some command, it makes a point of speaking of some divine attribute in that context. It reinforces the point that a particular command or duty incumbent upon man proceeds from that particular divine attribute. One who discharges *Sharī'ah* duties with this realization that such and such duty refers to a particular divine attribute recognizes the essence of *Sharī'ah*. In acting upon *Sharī'ah* commands with this knowledge one can understand what divine attributes are reflected in them. The Prophet Muḥammad (peace and blessings be upon him) termed this as *iḥsān*. In other words, one obeys Allah as if he sees Allah. This seeing consists in his perception of some divine attribute in every *Sharī'ah* command. He is filled with the realization that Allah's watchful eyes observe him.

As the believer recites the Qur'ān, he will become aware that every command or note of guidance is followed by the reference to some divine attribute. An observation is followed by the affirmation that Allah is All-Knowing and All-Aware; a command by the affirmation that Allah is All-Knowing and All-Wise. Similarly, a prohibition is followed by the warning that Allah is All-Mighty and All-Powerful. This gives us assurance that *Sharī'ah* represents a manifestation of divine attributes. One who follows *Sharī'ah* strictly follows the way of Allah. Implicit in this is the point that only those can appreciate the essence of *Sharī'ah* commands who perceive divine attributes in them. Those unable to do so have only a formal religious outlook, devoid of any stability or vitality.

A common misconception

It is imperative at this point to draw attention to a common misconception. It is one thing to fulfill the obligations proceeding from divine attributes and quite another to strive to be an incarnation of divinity. The latter is patently false and un-Islamic. *Sharī'ah* helps man maintain his ties with Allah and the underlying objective is that, both outwardly and inwardly, he should discharge the obligations necessitated by divine attributes. Man's perfection consists in his striving for this goal in accordance with *Sharī'ah*. As it is, Messengership represents perfection. However, it is not something which can be acquired. It is a divine favour. Allah elevates to this exalted rank whom He wills.

However, the goal of mysticism, as represented by certain ascetics and especially its pantheistic variety, is not to adapt oneself to divine attributes. Rather, they mistakenly aspire to be an incarnation of the divine. Their disciplines are not geared towards behaving as perfect servants of Allah, but to acquire divine attributes and to merge with the divine. This stance is at odds with *Sharī'ah*. For *Sharī'ah* aims only at rendering man into a perfect and obedient servant of Allah. The self-development recommended by *Sharī'ah* is geared towards this same goal. The practitioners of false mysticism, however, try to approximate divinity. They are mistaken in both their conception and their execution. Some ascetics think that since Allah is independent, they too should strive for independence. Likewise, they seek to imitate other divine attributes such as those of self-sufficiency and knowledge, especially knowledge of the unseen. They exert themselves to attain these attributes by undergoing spiritual exercises. Some of them would like to develop the healing touch, which is special to Allah alone. Others try to resurrect the dead, or to exercise authority over elements of nature. Even when they discharge *Sharī'ah* obligations, their motives are false and un-Islamic. For them, these *Sharī'ah* obligations are the means for achieving objectives. At some stage, they are willing to violate all *Sharī'ah* restrictions, considering them negatively as a barrier to their pursuits.

Islam rejects this false concept of man's relationship with Allah. On man's relation with Allah, the basic Islamic principle is that man should do his best to act in line with divine attributes. Since Allah is generous, man should devote all his energy to behave as His most grateful servant. As Allah is the Creator, man must make it a point to obey all His commands. By the same token, since Allah is All-Hearing and All-Knowing, man should invoke only Him and repose all trust in Him. In recognition of the truth that

Allah is the All-Holy, one should purify oneself both outwardly and inwardly. Since Allah is the judge and All-Mighty, man should shun any injustice out of fear of Him. In sum, each and every divine attribute places certain obligations on man. The more man advances in this direction, the nearer he reaches Him. This elevation makes his role more difficult and challenging.

We drew attention to this important point before proceeding further in our main discussion on self-development in view of the fact that the evil influence of false mysticism has crept, in a certain degree, into Sufism which is professed and practised by some Muslims. Until this misconception is removed, we cannot appreciate fully the nature of the self-development recommended by the Qur'ān and the *Sunnah*. We shall draw upon various elements and features of this self-development in the following pages.

We value greatly the works by classical scholars on Sufism. However, notwithstanding our respect for these distinguished authors, we feel at places that their interpretation of certain things is not substantiated by the Qur'ān and the *Sunnah*. On testing their formulations against the touchstone of the Qur'ān and the *Sunnah*, we note in many instances that their stance is not in line with *Sharī'ah*. By their standards even the Companions do not measure-up. This has a demoralizing effect, leaving the odd impression that *Sharī'ah* obligations are not practicable or that man cannot meet these in any degree. It projects a false, misleading concept about humanness. Therefore, we thought it proper to issue the above note of warning about Sufism.

These introductory remarks are followed by a fuller elaborate discussion of the basis of man's relationship with Allah, as presented in the Qur'ān. We can fulfill our obligations within that relationship as we appreciate the essence of divine attributes.

GRATITUDE

Gratitude lies at the core of man's relationship with Allah. It may be expressed by the heart, tongue, through deeds, words and gestures. As to the gratitude flowing from the heart, it is the proper response for innumerable divine favours. A grateful person is always mindful of being indebted for Allah's bounties, big and small, and articulates his feelings at every step to express gratitude.

This feeling of constant gratitude has a very significant bearing on man's deeds. For he is pleased to do the deeds that please Allah, his benefactor. Conversely, he is averse to anything that amounts to ingratitude in response to a divine bounty. One who truly appreciates divine bounties can never reconcile himself to abusing them by acting against Allah's will. If someone gives us a weapon that can help us to defend ourselves, only a wicked person would abuse that weapon to hurt the one who gave it. One who truly appreciates divine bounties is never ready to abuse them in the cause of Satan. Umm al-Mu'minīn 'Ā'ishah made this point in her letter to Amīr Mu'āwiyah: 'A person blessed with some favour owes the minimum obligation of not abusing that favour against his benefactor.'

To develop a constant feeling of gratitude and a sound consciousness on this count, the first and foremost task is to constantly acknowledge and declare the favours bestowed upon one by Allah. It is a general human weakness that if someone is afflicted with some misfortune, he is continually mentioning it to others. However, he does not declare the numerous bounties which he constantly enjoys. He disregards these as if these do not exist. Such a person is not likely to appreciate the favours done to him by his benefactor. To overcome this weakness, we should devote a little time every day to reflect on the bounties we enjoy and to study divine signs scattered around us. We should reflect too on what our state would be if he had not been blessed by Allah with the favours we are currently enjoying. If we had not been endowed with eyes, ears, limbs and brain, we would not have been able to accomplish anything. We would have led a miserable life.

Another equally important point to remember is that Allah has granted us innumerable favours even though we have not deserved them. By definition, Allah is not obliged to do us these favours, and we can never repay Him in any measure for His bounties. While we cannot repay Him, He can deprive us of His favours whenever He wills, and there is no one to stop Him from doing so. A king may be reduced to a pauper; so he should not dismiss a lowly person, for Allah may degrade us to the same position. However, as we enjoy a privilege, respectable position, we should be grateful to Him for His grace and mercy. We should constantly praise Him for His favours to us.

Another help in encouraging gratitude is not to look at those who have been blessed with more than us, but at those who have been blessed with less. Those who fail to do this are always complaining of their difficulties and problems, and are never blessed with satisfaction or contentment. Even when their lot improves, they do not experience true contentment. This is because it is impossible to be in a state that is in all respects better than that of everyone else. The only way to express our gratitude to Allah is to be constantly mindful that we are the servants of Allah – some of His servants are not granted as much as we have, and others are favoured with more than us.

The wisdom in that approach is well illustrated by an anecdote related by Shaikh Sa'dī. While travelling he reached Damascus in a miserable condition. He did not have any money to buy new shoes to replace his old ones. It pained him that he was unable to buy a pair of new shoes. With these thoughts he entered the mosque where he observed a lame person, without feet. On seeing this, he immediately fell into prostration, thanking Allah profusely for having provided him with feet, if not with new shoes. This incident identifies the perspective in which we should look at things. Those with a feeling of gratitude observe numerous manifestations of Allah's favours, which then fill them with greater gratitude. However, there are others who are always complaining of what they do not have, and are therefore unable to thank Allah for the many blessings He has bestowed upon them.

WORSHIP

The other fundamental component of man's relationship with Allah is worship. As one's heart is filled with gratitude to one's benefactor, one expresses indebtedness, humility and surrender to him. This is a natural response, observed even in domestic animals and pets. They express gratitude by gesture or look, but human beings are required to express gratitude in a much more pronounced manner. It is ordinary experience that a person owing a debt of gratitude to another expresses his feelings in appropriate manners and speech. Those failing to thank their benefactor are generally regarded as at least uncouth or ill-natured. It is part of the human nature to hold one's benefactor in esteem. Given this, we can see what gratitude we owe to our true benefactor, Allah, Who is the source of all favours and blessings. We owe our very existence to Him. His favours are not ephemeral, but eternal. Man should reflect his gratitude to Allah by way of surrendering himself humbly and fully to Him. In so doing, man acts in a natural way, and will be blessed with tranquillity and spiritual contentment. However, those overwhelmed by neglect or ignorance fail to give thanks to their Creator and Benefactor. We pointed earlier to man's indifference and neglect on this count. As to his ignorance, it consists in mistaking the means as his real benefactor. He fails to even think of his real benefactor, or does so only in a passing and cursory manner.

The gratitude we owe to Allah is manifested in our worship. It is expressed both verbally and by gesture and body movement. Worship embodies outwardly our gratitude to our benefactor. Man's whole being is involved in the act of worship. Each body part contributes in its own way, and his mental and spiritual faculties are also actively involved. Man's whole being takes part in paying homage to his Creator, because it is incumbent upon him to involve also all those means and ways to which he resorts for meeting his worldly needs.

There is no need of weighty argument to illustrate that the worship of Allah manifests our gratitude to our real, true benefactor. This appears clearly in the opening *surah* of the Qur'ān, *al-Fātiḥah*. The *surah* is woven around the theme of gratitude and it forms an essential part of prayer in Islam. It emerges from studying this *surah*, that man's gratitude in response to Allah's lordship, mercy and compassion, prompts him to exclaim: 'We worship You alone.' It is evident from other Qur'ānic passages also that worship is synonymous with the expression of gratitude to Allah. For example, 'Worship Allah and be His grateful servants.' (al-Zumar 39:66) Elsewhere man is directed to worship and thank Him (al-'Ankabūt 29:17). It is reported about the Prophet Muḥammad (peace and blessings be upon him) that he stood for so long in his night prayers that his feet would swell up. Take the following *ḥadīth* as illustrative: 'Umm al-Mu'minīn 'Ā'ishah says: I asked: O Messenger of Allah! Why do you exert yourself so much while all your sins have been forgiven? To this he replied: O 'Ā'ishah! Should I not be a grateful servant of Allah.' (Muslim)

Worship is prompted by one's feeling of gratitude to Allah. In asking us to worship Him, Allah does not intend to put us to any inconvenience. Rather, He has prescribed certain forms for expressing our gratitude and these forms are approved by Him. These accrue numerous blessings to us. In terms of its essence true worship is characterized by genuine and overflowing gratitude to Allah – an act of worship devoid of this feeling and performed merely as a ritual, is not accepted by Allah. By worshipping Allah man discharges his obligations towards his Creator, Master, Benefactor and Lord. He does not do so for the sake of benefiting in any way his Creator and Master. Rather, he earns blessings for himself and makes himself worthy of more rewards. It is clear from several Qur'ānic verses that Allah is to be worshipped because He is the Creator, Master and Sustainer and Lord. Our worship does not profit Him in any way, and our refusal to worship Him does not harm Him in the least. However, the unbelievers refusing to worship Him are liable to fall more deeply into error and more likely to prefer the path of Satan than the straight way prescribed by Allah.

OBEDIENCE

As well as worshipping Allah, the Muslim should obey Him in all aspects of life in order to maintain a healthy, vibrant relationship with Him. In Islam Allah is not entitled only to some formal rites, the mistaken view of some of the followers of Hinduism and Christianity. On the contrary, man owes total obedience and commitment to Allah. What this signifies is that he should faithfully obey all the laws laid down by Allah and communicated by His Messenger. These laws seek to perfect man's individual and collective life.

Reason demands that man obey divine commands unquestioningly. For it makes little sense that one recognizes Allah as worthy of worship, and yet feels he can disregard His commands, or even deny them altogether. It is unthinkable that Allah, being the Lord, would not instruct man how to lead his life. Since He has promulgated certain laws, it is common sense that man obeys them. For Allah is entitled to all worship and obedience. Offering worship to one, and obedience to another, is plainly contradictory. To reconcile oneself to such an absurd position is nonsensical.

Islam requires that man should manifest his obedience to Allah. Those who have studied Islam know well that Allah does not simply require that man worship Him. Rather, He makes it a point that man also obeys Him. Accordingly Allah instructs that man should do the prayers and obey Him. As well as instructing man in offering prayers, fasting and paying *zakāh,* Allah asks man to abide by His commands in mutual dealings in business and trade, agriculture, commerce and political life. The Qur'ānic commands on a wide range of issues are meant to be implemented. If they were not meant to be enforced, it would be pointless to have stated them. The Qur'ān declares: 'And whoever does not judge by what Allah has sent down, they are unbelievers'; 'And whoever does not judge according to what Allah has sent down, they are wrongdoers'; 'And whoever does not judge according to what Allah has sent down, they are ungodly.' (al-Mā'idah 5:44, 45, 47) Because the Qur'ān does not ask man merely to worship Him but repeatedly commands him to obey Allah, we must affirm that the divine laws must be implemented: 'Say: "Obey Allah and the Messenger." Then, if they turn away, surely Allah does not love unbelievers.' (Āl 'Imrān 3:32); 'O you who believe! Obey Allah and obey the Messenger and those charged with authority among you.' (al-Nisā' 4:59) The practical manifestation of obedience to Allah is in obedience to the Messenger. For it is he who, acting as His messenger, instructs man in divine commands and works for their implementation. It is not surprising therefore that the Qur'ānic directive to obey Allah is immediately conjured with the exhortation to abide by the Prophet's instructions. As far as man's obedience is concerned Islam does not admit any distinction between Allah and His Messenger. As for those who recognize their subservience to Allah yet refuse to obey the Messenger, they betray their defiance of Allah's will as communicated by His messenger. No legal system allows the authority of its representatives or agents to be divided or rejected. Thus, Allah rules out, in respect of injunctions to be obeyed, any distance between His will and the commands of His Messenger: 'By your Lord, they shall not truly believe until they have made you judge of what is disputed among them, and then find no demur in their hearts against what you have decreed and they submit with full submission.' (al-Nisā' 4:65)

Allah does not sanction any deviation from obedience to Him, except in the following two cases – sheer forgetfulness, or being controlled by overwhelming desires. As to the former, one should seek His forgiveness and repent sincerely. For remedying the latter one should try to improve one's conduct. Otherwise, a person who refuses to obey Allah strikes at the very roots of his relationship with Him.

Wherever Muslims are in a position to enforce Allah's commands, they are obliged to do so and abide by them. A way of life based on the instructions of Allah and His messenger is decidedly the best. Those at the helm of affairs in such a system occupy the position of representatives of the Messenger. Accordingly, they command our obedience. The reference in the Qur'ān quoted above (al-Nisā' 4:59), is to such persons of authority. Those who defy them are guilty of disobeying Allah and His Messenger. It is reported on the authority of Abū Hurairah that the Prophet (peace and blessings be upon him) said:

'Whoever obeys me, in fact, obeys Allah. Likewise, he who follows those in authority, he obeys me. Whoever disobeys me is guilty of disobeying Allah. Likewise, he who defies those in authority disobeys me.' (Ibn Mājah)

The above *Hadīth* makes it plain that in the Islamic scheme of things, obedience to Allah, His Messenger and those in authority in an Islamic order, are synonymous. One who refuses to obey the Messengers defies Allah; similarly those who refuse to follow the legitimate Islamic authority are guilty of disobeying Allah. These three manifestations of authority are intertwined, though they appear as three distinct entities. For all practical purposes they represent a unified whole. For the overall objective is to obey Allah while the Messenger and those in authority are the means to it.

Islam, no doubt, accords an exalted position to those in authority. It is done in recognition of their total obedience to Allah and their efforts to enforce divine commands in the society. For the Prophet Muḥammad (peace and blessings be upon him), the most important thing was that men obey Allah's commands. Conversely, he did not approve of those who violated divine commands. Those in authority are therefore obliged not to deviate even slightly from divine commands. Nor should they ask people to do something which is contrary to a divine command. They should be constantly aware that Allah represents the true and real authority and that men are obliged to obey Him, whereas they are, at most, in their capacity as agents for His authority, responsible for commanding their obedience to Him. It is not proper on their part to issue a command which contravenes the command of the true authority. If they ever do so, they forego their legitimacy as Islamic rulers.

Allah's commands are both hard and easy. At times, one faces great hardships in abiding by these. However, Allah demands of His servants that they should always follow His directives. Allah does not accept the conduct of those who obey Him only in such matters as suit them and who seek a way out in matters in which their interests clash with divine commands. They incur His wrath and curse. The Jews stand out as an illustration of such misconduct among earlier communities. For they tampered with divine *Sharī'ah* in such matters as did not suit their interests. They tried to adapt *Sharī'ah* to the challenges of their time. However, their interpolations were not accepted by Allah. In punishment for their outrageous misconduct He deprived them of His *Sharī'ah* and inflicted upon them His curse.

SINCERITY

Allah accepts only those acts of worship and other rituals that are characterized by sincerity. What this means is that one should perform a deed only for the sake of earning Allah's pleasure. One should not be prompted by any other motive.

Although sincerity has been variously defined, the essence of it is conveyed by the definition above. A mystic has defined sincerity that one's objective in obeying should be for Allah's pleasure. According to another authority, it consists in being indifferent to other motivations. It is defined also in terms of consistency between one's inward and outward condition. One should be so devoted to Allah that one disregards public criticism. In the words of Fuḍayl ibn 'Iyāḍ, avoiding a sin with a view to defending oneself against public criticism betrays hypocrisy. A sincere person is one who is devoted heart and soul to Allah. This is evident from the definition appearing in these *aḥādīth*:

> 'Umar ibn al-Khaṭṭāb reports that he heard the Prophet (peace and blessings be upon him) say: 'The reward of deeds depends upon the intentions and every person will get the reward according to what he intended. So whoever emigrated for worldly benefits or for a woman to marry, his emigration was for what he emigrated for.' (Bukhārī and Muslim)

It is reported on the authority of Abū Mūsā 'Abdullāh ibn Qais al-Ashʿarī that someone asked the Prophet (peace and blessings be upon him) that if one takes part in war for making a show of his bravery while another is motivated only by religious considerations, who will be taken as a fighter in Allah's cause? To this he replied: 'One who fights for the cause of Allah and for upholding His word is the one who fights in His way.' (Bukhārī and Muslim)

In another *ḥadīth* it is asserted that hellfire will be kindled first for the following three kinds of persons: (1) Those who recite the Qur'ān for the sake of being known as reciters of the Qur'ān, (2) Those fighters who participate in *jihād* in order to gain fame as *mujāhids* (3) And those who give in charity to gain a reputation as generous persons. (Tirmidhī)

The Qur'ān offers the following definition of sincerity and brings out its significance in the following verses:

And they were commanded not but they should worship Allah keeping the *Dīn* pure for Him, as upright people (al-Bayyinah 98:5).

'Worship Allah, offering Him sincere devotion. Is it not to Allah that sincere devotion is due?' (al-Zumar 39:2-3)

'Say: It is Allah I worship, making faith for Him exclusive. So worship whatever you will besides Him.' (al-Zumar 39:14-15)

'Say: Truly my prayers and my service of sacrifice and my life and my death are all for Allah, Lord of the worlds. No associate has He. To this I am bidden, and I am the first of those who submit.' (al-Anʿām 6:162-163)

An essential condition of sincerity is that one should perform a deed only for the sake of Allah. Another equally important element is that the deed should be consonant with Allah's command and the *Sunnah*. These two qualities are integral to sincerity. If a person does something for Allah, but the act is contrary to the command of Allah and His Messenger, it cannot be sincere, since it amounts to showing disrespect to Allah and His Messenger. For it implies that he claims to possess a better understanding of divine commands than what is declared by Allah and His Messenger. This misconception is rooted in pride and polytheism. Therefore any act which violates a divine command cannot have any sincerity, even if it is done with the utmost devotion.

The following observation by Fuḍayl ibn ʿIyāḍ is worthy of note. On being asked to define an excellent deed, he remarked: 'An excellent deed is characterized by sincerity and altruism. Moreover, it should have a sense of purpose.' When he was requested to clarify further, he said that a deed is not accepted by

Allah if it lacks sincerity. It should be only for the sake of Allah, and sound in itself in that it should conform to the *Sunnah*. He recited some Qur'ānic verses in order to substantiate his observation.

If a deed were acceptable by Allah on the grounds of the doer's total commitment, then monasticism would have secured His approval. Indeed, Allah speaks of the sincerity of those who introduced monasticism. However, notwithstanding their sincerity, their monasticism is dismissed as a false innovation. It troubles some people that a good deed is not accepted, if it is not done for the sake of Allah or if one associates others with Him. For is it not a good deed in itself? This apprehension betrays an ignorance of the fundamental truth of faith. Allah does not stand in need of man's good or bad deeds. He does not need people to do good for Him, nor is He obliged to them for their good deeds. It is not binding upon Him to appreciate every good deed and recompense it, if that deed runs counter to His will.

Allah might have peopled the earth only with angels. In that case there would not be anyone on the face of the earth who could commit an evil deed. He might have created everyone pious, unable to commit sin. Notwithstanding His absolute power to do so, Allah has not arranged the world in this way. For He does not seek only good deeds and piety. What He wants is that man should do good deeds only to attain His pleasure and in accordance with His command. He places great value on good deeds that meet these conditions, even if they are minor and He rewards them lavishly. However, there is no divine reward for a deed which is adulterated with some base motive. He asks such people to seek their reward from those for whom they did their deeds. In the following *ḥadīth qudsī* it is affirmed: 'I am independent of associates. So if anyone does a deed, while associating others with Me, I disregard it. That deed is only for the one person for whom it is done.' (Ibn Mājah) When such people claim reward, He will direct them to those for whom they had done what they did. He will not grant them any reward.

Idols, family, tribe or nation can be such associates. Desire for fame and other base motives can also be associates. Whatever they may be, associates negate the spirit of sincerity and render one's deeds false and vain in the sight of Allah.

This should not, however, give rise to the misunderstanding that a sincere Muslim should not do anything for his family, tribe or nation. For Allah has specified clearly the obligations one owes in this regard. It is obligatory on every Muslim to discharge these duties in order to earn His pleasure in line with His commands. One who does so is entitled to generous reward from Allah. However, if it is not done for the sake of Allah, it betrays mere worldliness. As already noted, even *jihād* falls into this category, if it is not waged sincerely.

On a little reflection it appears that sincerity or its lack have an important bearing on the thrust of one's deeds. A mother has tremendous love and affection for her baby. Yet, if she over-feeds the baby, or feeds it indiscriminately against medical advice, it will lead only to harming the baby, perhaps its death. Likewise, if a person does good deeds without the sole objective of pleasing Allah, he will be drawn to fake criteria of good and evil, and the outcome of his actions will increase the spread of evil. While working for the interest of his tribe and nation, he will ultimately follow the principle: 'My country first, right or wrong.' This attitude degenerates into fascism of the Hitler and Mussolini variety. However, if he is prompted by the ideal of pleasing Allah alone he will not deviate from the right way. For this objective gives his motives and actions a universal perspective, and he will be engaged in serving all mankind even as he works for the interest of his nation.

Thus, Islam forbids man to take anyone besides Allah as the ideal. This constitutes the essence of sincerity. It underlies the doctrine of monotheism, which is the ground of Muslim relationship with Allah.

LOVE

To meet the demands of faith, it is not enough to worship and obey Allah. Rather, worship and obedience should be tempered with genuine love for Allah. For without love, worship and obedience may degenerate into hypocrisy, which is not acceptable to Allah. He does not stand in need of any of our deeds. On the contrary, He accepts only those deeds that are done exclusively for Him and are characterized with a strong love for Him. Love for Him should surpass one's love for other worldly things. The Qur'ān sets the following standard:

'Say: If your father and your sons and your brothers and your wives and your family and the riches you have acquired and the trade in which you fear a slackening and the dwellings which please you are dearer to you than Allah and His Messenger and striving in His cause, then wait until He brings about His decree; and Allah does not guide the ungodly people.' (al-Tawbah 9:24)

The same point is reiterated in *aḥādīth*: 'The Prophet (peace and blessings be upon him) observed that one's faith is not genuine unless one holds him dearer than family, possessions and all else.' (Muslim) In some variant reports of this *ḥadīth* mention is made of Allah and His Messenger as one's most precious possession.

It is reported on the authority of Anas that the Prophet (peace and blessings be upon him) said: 'One can taste true faith, if he is characterized with the following: (1) if he holds Allah and His Messenger dearer than all else; (2) if he loves someone only for the sake of Allah; and (3) if he abhors unbelief after having attained deliverance in the same measure as he avoids jumping into fire.' (Muslim)

A query and its clarification

Some people ask whether it is at all possible to love someone that one has never seen and whether that love can surpass his love for all else. The answer to this question is that it is more than possible, it is innately in man to love what is unseen. He does not love what he observes serving him day and night such as his own body parts. He stands in need of their smooth functioning for his well-being. However, if asked to make a choice, he will forego all his physical faculties in preference to his mental faculty, though the latter is something invisible and imperceptible. What explains this is that although man has not seen his own mental faculty, he realizes that it represents that which accounts for his excellence and dignity. If he is deprived of other physical faculties, he will still enjoy that dignity. However, if he is stripped of his mental faculty, he will be reduced to an animal, commanding no respect or honour.

The above point holds true for all the objects in the universe. Man benefits from innumerable objects of nature, day and night. However, he knows that these do not serve him on their own. On the contrary, the Supreme Being has assigned them the duty to serve him. He knows well that he has not created and cannot create any of these objects. Furthermore, he is not entitled to their subservience. Since he recognizes that he owns everything as a result of the favour and grace shown by the Supreme Being and that He can withdraw these at any time, it fills his heart with overflowing gratitude to Allah. This prompts him to love Him more than all else.

It is not therefore correct to hold that man cannot love Allah. Allah is no doubt invisible yet His manifestations are too evident. Man observes these all around himself. Each object of nature, be it the clouds, winds, rivers and mountains, points to His existence. Birds sing in praise of Him and trees share this hymn. His signs are embedded in each and every particle of dust, and in every leaf. Far from being hidden, Allah is manifest, evident everywhere. Man suffers from such misperception if he fails to recognize this evident truth. As a result, he does not develop any love for Him. This, in turn, divests man of His love.

Love for Allah is essential for gaining gnosis

One thus learns that Allah's invisibility is not an obstacle to man's love for Him. Rather, it is man who nurtures misapprehensions about Him, which at times result in severing his relationship with Allah. At times, man suffers serious misperceptions about Allah's power and knowledge. He mistakenly thinks that Allah has delegated His authority to helpers and associates. Therefore, apart from worshipping Him, man engages in worshipping those whom he regards as His associates. His love for them exceeds his love for Allah. In this mistaken belief he depends upon them for meeting his needs. Likewise, if man does not have a correct understanding of Allah's justice, he suffers from the delusion that Allah does not make any discrimination between good and evil. Or he tends to think that some beings are His favourites and that his devotion to them will help him earn Allah's pleasure and his deliverance in the Hereafter, without reference to his own deeds. Accordingly, in preference to Allah, he devotes himself heart and soul to these supposed favourites of Allah and his devotion to them constitutes his faith.

There are many who are ignorant of the divine dispensation about man's adversity and prosperity. Accordingly, they grow indifferent to Him or despair of His mercy. For example, Allah bestows His favours upon some in order to see whether they grow more grateful or act arrogantly. Those not familiar with this divine dispensation misinterpret divine favours. Likewise, Allah puts some to a trial in order to test their perseverance. If they do not appreciate the spirit of this divine law, they tend to think that Allah has abased them. Consequently they despair of His grace. These misperceptions drive one to even committing polytheism. One is enmeshed in Satan's snares. The only way out for man is to seek perfect gnosis of Allah, which may defend him against Satan's prompting. It is not easy to shut the door completely upon Satan. However, by developing a perfect gnosis of Allah, people can defend themselves against Satan's attack. As to those attracted towards Satan, no one can redeem them.

While speaking of gnosis, we do not imply any mystical connotation. This gnosis consists in developing a correct understanding of the Qur'ān and the *Ḥadīth*. Owing to the constraints of space, it is not possible to spell out all its details. We shall therefore restrict ourselves to pointing to certain fundamental principles.

The most definite and reliable means for gaining gnosis of Him is to grasp His names and attributes, which He has described in His Book. He knows best His attributes. He instructs man not to interfere in this matter. The Qur'ān warns: 'Do not invent similitudes for Allah.' (al-Naḥl 16:74) In the following supplication recommended by the Prophet Muḥammad (peace and blessings be upon him), one is instructed to acknowledge one's ignorance in respect of comprehending the attributes of Allah: 'O Allah! I cannot fully glorify You. For You are as perfect as You have described Yourself.' (Muslim)

If man is given an option to invent divine attributes, he is liable to create an idol of his choice and be subservient to his desires. His whole concept of faith will be altered accordingly. On studying the history of religions it emerges that the mistake in the concept of God lies at the heart of all fallacies. It is therefore imperative that one gains a true understanding of divine attributes.

A proper understanding of the concept of Allah enables one to determine what pleases and angers Him. One appreciates His power, Lordship, mercy and wisdom which permeate the believer's faith, giving him perseverance and consistency. It inspires him to withstand all the challenges in life. More importantly, it infuses into him such deep-rooted fear of Allah that even while he is alone and he does not see Allah, he realizes that his actions and conduct are being watched by Him. This in turn strengthens his conviction in monotheism and the realization that no one can grant him anything, if Allah does not will it and that no one can withhold what Allah has ordained for him. He comes to understand therefore that Allah deals with His servants with perfect justice, knowledge and mercy. For no one dare utter a single word in His presence without His leave. Furthermore, it contributes to his self-development in that he gains a clear idea of his shortcomings by realizing what acts are acceptable to his Creator and what Allah dislikes. We must be ever mindful of the basic truth that all sound knowledge and *Sharī'ah* derive from a proper understanding of divine attributes. For these guide one to true knowledge and understanding.

Way to gaining the gnosis of Allah

Let us now reflect on the question how to gain the gnosis of Allah properly. Classical scholars have dwelt at length on this issue. Mention should be made of Imām Ghazālī's discussion on this issue in his *Iḥyā' al-'Ulūm al-Dīn*. His account is both comprehensive and insightful. Sufi masters have expressed a wide range of views on the subject. To the best of our knowledge however, the best account is provided by Imām Ibn Qayyim in his *Madārij al-Sālikīn*. The way suggested by him is rooted in the Qur'ān, the *Sunnah*, common sense and human nature. Reproduced below is a summary of his account. He recommends that one should take the following ten steps to develop true love for Allah:

1. Studying the Qur'ān with full concentration, with a view to fathoming its meaning and message.

2. Observing regularly both the obligatory and additional duties in order to gain nearness to Allah. This elevates one's status in the sight of Allah.

3. Remembering Allah consistently, no matter whatever one's condition. This remembrance should be evident from one's tongue, heart, deeds and manners. The more one remembers Him, the stronger the love one will develop for Him.

4. Striving to do what is commanded by Allah in preference to one's own desires. One should not give up in this pursuit, notwithstanding the hardships faced.

5. Studying consistently Allah's names and attributes, observing His wondrous signs and valuing gnosis. One who recognizes Allah with reference to His names, attributes and accomplishments is bound to develop a strong love for Him. By contrast those who deny His attributes fail to have any love for Him.

6. Constantly taking note of Allah's numerous favours and bounties and His glory and majesty. This generates a strong love for Him.

7. Above all, surrendering oneself wholly to Him in all humility. This inner condition cannot be adequately described in words.

8. Making it a point to supplicate earnestly to Allah, to recite His Book and to stand before Him while observing all the norms of servitude to Him. It should be characterized by constant seeking of forgiveness and repentance.

9. Joining the company of those who sincerely love Him, drawing upon their pious sayings, and not speaking unless one is persuaded that such speech will lead to one's own self-development and help others.

10. Avoiding all that acts as a barrier between his heart and his Lord.

While concluding this account, Imām Ibn Qayyim observes that the above way guides the seekers of truth to a deep love for Allah. In our considered opinion, his observation is perfectly right, because this way is rooted in the Qur'ān and the *Sunnah*.

A practical way to achieve love for Allah

Imām Ibn Qayyim's account is an academic approach. The Qur'ān shows us the practical way that can be easily followed by everyone, namely the way of the Prophet Muḥammad (peace and blessings be upon him). In him Allah presented the one who loved Him perfectly. Following him as role model, we can observe how a lover of Allah led his life in the company of his family and friends. His life stands out as the most practicable way in that it presents a living example. Allah observes: 'Say: If you love Allah, follow me [so] that Allah may love you and forgive your sins.' (Āl 'Imrān 3:31)

The Prophet (peace and blessings be upon him) stands as the best model for the love for Allah. No one can excel him in this regard. Those familiar with his sayings know well that whenever someone transgressed in this matter, he checked him immediately, saying that he loved and feared Allah most. Given this, one should not do something which may mark a deviation from his practice, whose every action was characterized by the perfect measure of devotion and piety.

An important warning

It is worth clarifying that we have employed the expression 'love' throughout this discourse. We have not used any other expression. For it is love which is used in this context in the Qur'ān and the *Sunnah*. Anything other than love betrays imbalance hence it cannot be used in the context of Allah and His Messenger. Furthermore, it constitutes disrespect towards them. Man's dealings with Allah and His Messenger are governed by *Sharī'ah* norms. Any deviation, even if it is prompted by a pious intention, results only in innovation and error. Poets and Sufi masters have carelessly used other expressions in this context. Poets are given to exaggeration. Even when they do not offer prayers and fasting, they make tall claims about their love for Allah and His Messenger. Each one of them pretends to be a lover of the Messenger. Sufi masters, too, are guilty of imbalance. Dissatisfied with the use of love in this context, they adopted the expression *'ishq'* (infatuation or extreme love) as rather more than a mere synonym. Misled by their false notions they have introduced many innovations.

Love is not something that is beyond the governance of norms. Rather, it is to be pursued within certain parameters. The love of Allah serves as a touchstone for self-evaluation and for assessing others. The unmistakable test is that when the believer is faced with the option of a way which he likes, and which is preferred by his friends and relatives, but which is contrary to Allah's command, he should renounce it. Likewise, he should disregard a way which runs counter to *Sharī'ah*. If he accords greater importance to his own desires, it betrays his love for himself or for others, and the hollowness of his claim to faith. However, if he disregards all such options and unreservedly opts for the way prescribed by Allah, he is to be taken as a true and genuine lover of Allah, even if he never presumes to claim such a title for himself.

Love as defined above is to be reckoned in matters of faith and will have its bearing on one's success and rank in the Hereafter. The Qur'ān has already laid out the norms for it. Everyone can test himself against this criterion. As to those who make outward show of their love, there is no Qur'ānic criterion for measuring it. It is hard to say whether what they profess is genuine or not.

FEAR

As love for Allah is essential for faith, so too fear of Allah is integral to it. One's love for Allah should surpass one's love for everyone else; similarly, one should fear Allah most. The Qur'ān declares that true believers have a genuine, unshakeable love for Allah: 'Those who believe are strong in their love for Allah.' (al-Baqarah 2:165) In a similar vein, it chides those who are afraid of others besides Allah: 'Do you fear them? Allah alone is to be feared, if you are true believers.' (al-Tawbah 9:13) 'Do not fear the wrong-doers among them. Fear Me.' (al-Baqarah 2:150)

Why should one fear Allah?

Allah is not to be feared because He is some 'dreaded tyrant', as polytheists mistakenly hold. Nor is He so arbitrary that He may instantly destroy one with whom He is in the slightest displeased. Rather, in the light of His attributes which feature in the Qur'ān, He appears as the Most Loving, Trustworthy, and Supreme Being. Some of His attributes, no doubt, point to His might and terror. However, these underpin His omnipotence and authority to comfort the believers, and to serve as a warning and admonition to the unbelievers. These attributes are not to be misinterpreted in the sense that He is some 'dreaded tyrant'. Such a notion is contrary to the spirit of the Qur'ān. It is nonetheless true that the divine laws which originate from His perfect attributes are such that one entertains a genuine fear of Him.

Allah has described at length these attributes of His in the Qur'ān. Those who do not turn to the Qur'ān may lead a life of untroubled indifference. However, of those familiar with its meaning and message it is said: 'their sides quit their beds so that they call upon their Lord in fear and hope.' (al-Sajdah 32:16) They take every step in the full realization that they will be held accountable one day before their Master for all that they say and do. The Qur'ān thus makes plain that those servants of His most fear Him who possess the knowledge of His Book (Fāṭir 35:28). The 'possessing of knowledge' does not refer to the *ʿulamā'* in a narrow sense. It refers to those who possess true knowledge imparted by Allah and His Messenger. They are fully cognizant of the divine attributes, laws and commands. Accordingly they fear Him as He should be feared. As to those who are unaware of His attributes and laws, they have no reason to fear Him. At most they may take Him as an imaginary being and dread Him according to their horrible imagining. It is noteworthy that the Qur'ān makes it obligatory on the believers that they should fear Allah as He is to be feared (Āl 'Imrān 3:102). It is therefore all the more necessary to study the issue of the fear of Allah in the light of the Qur'ān in order to help the seekers of truth.

Real motives for fearing Allah

The first and foremost reason for fearing Allah, as this is described in the Qur'ān, is that Allah is All-Wise and that He has created the universe with a grand design and purpose. That purpose and design require that, on the Day of Judgement, He will reward the pious who led a life of virtue in this world and duly punish those who caused corruption and wickedness on earth. If He does not do so, it amounts to indifference towards good and evil, indifference towards whether man leads a life of obedience or rebellion. Such a presupposition negates the divine attributes of mercy, lordship, justice, power and wisdom. Accordingly, while addressing the unbelievers, the Qur'ān pointedly asks them whether they think that He has created them in vain and that they will not return to Him. Furthermore, it asks whether those gifted with knowledge and those who are ignorant are to be treated alike. In the absence of the Day of Judgement, everyone will be treated alike, reducing the whole universe and creation to a plaything. Islam does not admit any such fallacy. Rather, it asks every sane person to fear Allah's grip and punishment and to control his base self: 'They reflect upon the creation in the heavens and on earth. [Their supplication is:] "O Lord! You have not created this in vain. Glory and praise be to You, and protect us against the punishment of fire."'(Āl 'Imrān 3:191) As to those who take this universe and creation as a mere plaything and lead life fearlessly, they are bound to face the consequences of their foolishness.

Another reason which should make us fearful of Allah is that His grip is severe, not to be matched by the punishment inflicted by any tyrant on earth. For no one can punish in the manner Allah does. He defines Himself in these terms: 'So on that Day none shall torment any like His torment. Nor shall any bind like His binding.' (al-Fajr 89:25-26) The explanation is that any earthly punishment culminates, at most, with death, and is restricted to this life. With one's death one's agony will be over. However, in contrast, Allah's punishment is spread over eternity. It knows no end. Nor can anyone grant any reprieve. Moreover, it is not impossible to escape the punishment of an earthly authority. By contrast Allah's kingdom extends to every nook and corner of the universe. It is impossible for one to run away from His grip. This holds true in an equal measure for both *jinn* and men. Allah pronounces this truth thus: 'O assembly of *Jinn* and mankind! If you are able to pass out of the regions of the heavens and the earth, then do pass out, but you cannot pass out except with an authority.' (al-Raḥmān 55:33) There are numerous ways of getting away from the security system of worldly rulers and authorities. Even the highest security prisons cannot guarantee absolutely the confinement of inmates. In sharp contrast, the angel of death deputed by Allah does not spare anyone, even though he be inside a fortified palace. Allah has assigned such custodians over hell who are not moved by the pleadings of the convicts. Nor do they ever shirk from their duty: 'Over it are angels, stern, strong, they do not disobey Allah in what He commands them.' (al-Taḥrīm 66:6)

Another relevant point is that one may profit in this life by resorting to bribery, ransom or other unfair means. These cannot and will not avail one with regard to Allah. One will not possess anything to offer as a bribe on the Day of Judgement. The convicts would obviously like very much to offer their dearest possessions as ransom for securing their release. However, they will have nothing to offer. It will be the Day of Recompense. One will be rewarded or punished in relation to one's deeds alone (al-Ṭūr 52:21). As to the helplessness and plight of the convicts on the Day of Judgement, the Qur'ān provides the following graphic account: 'The guilty one would like to ransom himself from the torment of that day by offering his children, his wife and his brother, and his kin who sheltered him, and all those on the earth: so that this might deliver him. By no means!' (al-Ma'ārij 70:11-15)

Ignorant polytheists place a high value on their idols, saints and messengers to intercede for their deliverance. The polytheistic Arabs mistakenly believed that their idols and *jinn* whom they ardently worshipped, enjoyed proximity with Allah and that they would secure their release. It is a pity that many Muslims of our times suffer from a comparable delusion that their saints will carry them to Paradise and that Allah will oblige their saints by allowing them to enter Paradise, without any reference to their beliefs and practices. In other words, for them deliverance is not linked with a Messenger. Rather, they invest saints with such authority. As a result they grow indifferent to their religious duties. In so doing they betray their ignorance of divine laws about intercession. Otherwise, they would not have acted so recklessly as to jeopardize their prospects in the Hereafter. What follows below is an account of the Qur'ānic stance on intercession so that those who do not know may gain a true understanding of divine law about it.

We should begin with a firm realization that no one can utter a word without His leave, what to say of prevailing upon Him. Only those granted leave in advance by Him will be allowed to say something. This applies to everyone, including the angels who enjoy nearness to Him (al-Anbiyā' 21:27). They dare not initiate conversation with Him. This is true for the archangel Gabriel who does not speak unless Allah gives him leave. Since this restriction is applicable to the Prophets and Messengers, it is unthinkable that some saints should have some force to sway Allah to do something.

Also relevant is that those allowed to speak can only do so about the individual regarding whom the permission has been granted. They do not have the freedom to do more or other than this. The Qur'ān expresses this strongly: 'And in awe of Him they are fearful.' (al-Anbiyā' 21:28)

Moreover, those who have leave to speak will be able to state only the truth. Allah knows best everyone's condition. Therefore, the one interceding cannot plead that he knows the case of a certain person better than He does. Allah's knowledge embraces everyone while man possesses only such knowledge as is granted by Allah to him. Given this, no one can speak a falsehood in His presence.

The intercession will not transform truth into falsehood, or vice versa. One person's wrong will not be condoned under the influence of another's intercession – that would divest the creation of its very purpose, and runs counter to the glory and power of the All-Wise.

Man's deliverance is wholly contingent upon his deeds and Allah's mercy. It is not related in any way to intercession: 'Then whosoever has worked good of an atom's weight shall see it. And whosoever has worked ill of an atom's weight shall see it.' (al-Zalzalah 99:7-8)

It is clear from the divine pronouncement quoted above that intercession is not applicable in absolute terms, nor is it so effective as some mistakenly think. It will help only a few persons who are eligible for it under divine law of justice. It cannot and does not negate His justice which is the very basis of *Sharī'ah* and in the working of the universe.

Its impact on one's life

If one studies the Qur'ān with a view to appreciating the divine attributes of glory and dominion, His absolute power and authority over the universe and the manifestation of His justice in the history of earlier communities, his heart is filled with awe and dread. This awe and dread proceed from reflection and meditation. One is not filled with awe as one might be on suddenly seeing some fearful monster. That is why the consequence of our reflection is to turn to Allah with greater sincerity and urgency. We understand that it is Allah alone who can grant peace and refuge. The Prophet (peace and blessings be upon him) is on record invoking Allah in several *aḥādīth* in the following words: 'O Lord! I seek only with You refuge from You.' (Muslim) As a baby instinctively takes refuge in the lap of his mother, a sincere servant of Allah turns earnestly to Him for help, support and protection. As to those who seek refuge with someone other than Allah, they are guilty of the same sin as was committed by the disobedient son of the Prophet Noah (peace and blessings be upon him). When the Prophet (peace and blessings be upon him) directed him to board the ark in order to escape divine punishment, he arrogantly turned down the offer, saying that he would find shelter at the mountaintop. Obviously he could not escape divine punishment. For no mountain can protect one against Allah's punishment.

Another worthy aspect of the fear of Allah is that it makes one indifferent to all else. Indeed, one grows fearless of everyone. As one surrenders oneself to Allah, it provides such peace and satisfaction that one realizes that no other than Him can bring profit or harm. Nor can anyone withhold from us something that Allah intends to bestow, nor can anyone grant what Allah withholds. One who enjoys such peace of mind is like a king on earth. It is said of Paradise that those who dwell therein will not know fear or grief. This holds true also of the person who fears Allah in this world. For he is constantly mindful that one day he must render his account before his Lord. Far from demoralizing him, this fills his heart with contentment and tranquillity. It puts an end to all imaginary fear.

We have presented only two of the principal effects of the fear of Allah. This matter is addressed at length in the Qur'ān and the *Ḥadīth*; it is not possible to go into it fully here. We will try to explain the basic principles in the following pages and hope readers will be able to appreciate the finer details.

In the light of the Qur'ān and the *Ḥadīth* it appears that the fear of Allah makes the Muslim pious in his individual and personal life, compassionate in his family life, and a reformer in his social life. The Muslim who does not reflect these qualities may be lacking in fear of Allah, notwithstanding his claim to possess it, or he may be unfamiliar with the true meaning of the fear of Allah.

The following points should be fully grasped. That person may be reckoned as pious in his personal and individual life who observes divine instructions in even the innermost aspect of his life. For he knows well that he is not hidden from Allah, however well he may be hidden from other people. He does not give rein to his desires lest they lead him to transgress divine limits. Not only does he shun evil, he does not even approach it. He is guided by the Prophet's advice that a shepherd who drives his herd too close to a farm, runs the risk that his flock may trespass into the farm. He therefore ensures that his base desires are held firmly in check. The thought of answerability on the Day of Judgement constantly engages his mind. For he will be held responsible for his every word and deed. The Qur'ān says of such people: 'And as for him who dreaded standing before his Lord, and restrained his soul from desires: the Garden shall be his resort.' (al-Nāzi'āt 79:40-41)

Compassion in his family life does not mean pride in his family or lineage. On the contrary it means that the Muslim recognizes his role and responsibility as the head of the family, for whose conduct he will be held accountable. He will be interrogated about the moral training of every family member. Far from boasting of the large size of his family, he is constantly anxious about their safety and welfare, lest he might be held as a reckless head. He strives unceasingly to discharge his duties for the guidance of his family members. It is this alone that can save him from embarrassment and disgrace on the Day of Judgement. His dutiful attitude on this count will help him rise as the leader of the pious on the Day of Judgement. The Qur'ān recounts how they will respond to their responsibility: 'They will say: We too were once fearful in the midst of our household, ever in dread. Then, Allah was gracious to us, and protected us from the torment of the scorching [wind].' (al-Ṭūr 52:26-27) In other words, pious Muslims do not lead a carefree life. On the contrary, they are ever conscious that on the Day of Judgement, they will be held accountable for their good and evil deeds. If they discharge their duty well, they will be rewarded with entry to Paradise.

As for reform in social life, the God-fearing person knows only too well that his indifference to the community and their good and evil ways will have its adverse impact upon himself as well. For as a community incurs Allah's wrath for the corruption caused by it, even those are punished who are not directly engaged in that corruption. Their punishment is for their failure to curb those who caused corruption. The Divine Law regarding the communities that are punished in this world is that only those are spared who worked for reform, without any regard for the criticism and persecution which they faced. As for those who live in isolation and are pious in their personal life, they too, suffer divine punishment. This point is illustrated by the Prophet (peace and blessings be upon him) using the parable of people in a boat. If some individuals on board make a hole in the boat and the others do not prevent them, all will drown when the boat sinks.

The Qur'ān has prescribed norms for one's efforts for reform. Even when no one listens, one should continue the effort so that Allah may absolve him. The Qur'ān tells of a group of reformers that, when some of them argued that it was useless to carry on when no one listened, those gifted with knowledge affirmed:

'We should go ahead with our effort so that it may serve as our defence in the sight of Allah.' (al-A'rāf 7:164) We should keep on striving for social reform; that striving shows that we discharge our obligation. The duty of social reform is not to be taken lightly; we should devote ourselves to it heart and soul. Allah will absolve only those who carried out this mission in the face of dangers even at the risk of their lives.

An important warning

It is important to heed the warning of the need to maintain a proper balance between hope and fear; without that balance we cannot enjoy a perfect relationship with Allah. The Qur'ān stresses that this balance be maintained, urging the Muslims to invoke Allah, full of hope and fear (al-A'rāf 7:56).

The balance is essential in that if one is overwhelmed by fear of Allah, it may lead to despondency and the believer may be misled by Satan into cynicism. One may turn to others besides Him and fall a prey to polytheism. Exactly the same happened in the case of the *Banī Isrā'īl* who kept on committing crimes in the false belief that Allah would pardon them. For they suffered from the delusion that they were the chosen servants of Allah and that He would overlook their crimes. This misplaced hope in divine mercy leads to the false belief that the mere affirmation of certain articles of faith will ensure one's deliverance. Those suffering from this misconception give no importance to the record of their deeds and fail to link them with their deliverance.

MODESTY

Along with fear and love, modesty is another requisite of faith. The Prophet (peace and blessings be upon him) makes it plain that modesty is part of faith (Muslim). The reference is not to natural bashfulness which we profess and practise in our mutual relations, but to the modesty which man must practise in his relationship with Allah. Our modesty in our social relations is the source of the same. If we are not modest in our relationship with Allah, it will undermine modesty in other relationships, resulting in a loss of aesthetic beauty. It is no wonder that godless societies of our times now sanction outrageous acts that used to be unthinkable. We could cite some obscene legislation passed by the British Parliament, but modesty prevents us from doing so. Since these godless people draw only upon their customs and traditions, and are not governed by divine law in their public life, they could not withstand the public pressure and succumbed to the changing times. The Prophet (peace and blessings be upon him) had this in mind when he observed: 'If you are not shy of Allah, you are liable to do anything.' (Bukhārī) In other words, modesty in relation to Allah acts as a deterrent and forbids us from committing evil. In its absence man is liable to commit any monstrous obscenity.

As already indicated, modesty has a bearing on human life in a variety of ways and defends man against Satan's snares. In the following *ḥadīth*, the Prophet (peace and blessings be upon him) brings out its comprehensive function: 'It is reported on the authority of 'Abdullāh ibn Mas'ūd that the Prophet (peace and blessings be upon him) observed: "Be shy of Allah as you are obliged to do." When those present affirmed that they were modest, he said: "We should be grateful to Allah. We should be shy of Him in the manner befitting Him. One should be watchful of his mental faculties and the ideas which he entertains. One should keep an eye on one's stomach and what it consumes. Above all, one should be constantly mindful of one's death, the disintegration of one's body. Those seeking the Hereafter are not after the joys of this life. Those who behave thus are truly modest towards Allah, as they are obliged to be.'" (Tirmidhī)

Its main elements

Divine attributes infuse into one consciousness of the need to maintain modesty. One who possesses a true knowledge of these attributes has strong belief in these and feels genuinely shy of Allah. By contrast, those ignorant of divine attributes, or those who are not careful about paying heed to them, are not shy of Allah or fellow human beings. They are little better than animals who do not have any consciousness of modesty.

Let us illustrate the above point of how a correct perception of certain attributes infuses into man the virtue of modesty and its impact upon his conduct. Of all the divine attributes, the idea of His perfect knowledge makes one really conscious of his own conduct. The believer should be always mindful that Allah watches his each and every act (al-Nisā' 4:1). Likewise, one should have the conviction that He is aware of the treachery committed by the eyes and of the secrets within the breast (al-Mu'min 40:19). Also important is to realize that we are always accompanied by Allah. For He is present even in the secret councils conducted inside well-guarded private buildings: 'There is no whispering among three but He is their fourth, nor among five but He is their sixth, nor fewer nor more, but He is with them wheresoever they may be.' (al-Mujādilah 58:7) Evidently, those who believe in the import of that verse cannot commit any misdeed even in privacy which may embarrass them in the sight of Allah. For they cannot conceive of any place where they are not seen by Allah. This persuades them that any sin they commit is being observed by Allah. Only a pervert or fearless person could commit a crime while conscious of that reality. The Qur'ān, however, observes of some that they mean to do mischief even in the sight of Allah (al-Qiyāmah 75:5).

It is noteworthy that Allah is particularly affronted by infidelity. This is expressed also in the earlier Scriptures. Just as a man cannot endure adultery committed by his wife, Allah cannot tolerate His servants worshipping other than Him. In one of his sermons the Prophet (peace and blessings be upon him) said: 'O people of my community! Allah is very particular about it that any male or female servant of His commits fornication.' (*Muwaṭṭa'* of Imām Mālik) In the earlier Scriptures and the Qur'ān, fornication and polytheism are mentioned together as grave crimes. Fornication metaphorically stands for the infidelity committed against Allah.

We observe day and night numerous manifestations of Allah's glory and power. In the face of these we should not entertain any false notion about our own supremacy and greatness. Man is no more than a fly or an ant in this vast universe. The mountains around us are high in comparison to us; as compared to the oceans we scarcely have the weight of a drop. Given this, if we think highly of ourselves and walk around arrogantly, it is a sort of self-mockery. A parable tells of a fly that sat on the horn of a bull.

After some time the fly asked the bull whether it should move away lest its weight might burden the bull. They bull replied that it was unaware of the fly's existence and it was immaterial to it whether the fly sat there or not. The same is true in a measure for certain arrogant ones who attach too much importance to themselves. They walk arrogantly on earth and always speak in a harsh tone. While admonishing them Allah tells them: 'And do not strut on the earth insolently. You will not by any means rend the earth. Nor can you match the mountains in stature.' (al-Isrā' 17:37) Man stands nowhere in comparison to the numerous manifestations of Allah's power and glory. Therefore, he should become all the more modest and humble.

Man should take to heart the truth that all his faculties and resources are granted to him only by Allah. He is not the creator of any of these, nor possesses them except by His leave. If he realizes this he is less liable to commit ingratitude or disobedience or rebellion. For he cannot do anything without drawing upon the very resources granted by Allah. Man is favoured with these so that he may lead his life as a grateful, obedient servant of Allah. However, if he abuses these in favour of treachery and rebellion, it constitutes a heinous crime. So he should be constantly and profoundly aware that it is Allah Who has blessed him with these favours. The Qur'ān reiterates this truth at numerous places.

Some persons think very highly of their contribution to the faith. They mistakenly consider themselves as the ones who have done good to Allah and His Messenger. However, even the greatest sacrifice offered by them does not really belong to them. If they donate money in His cause, money was granted in the first place to them by Allah. If someone suffers the delusion that he earned his wealth by dint of his talents and skills, he should not forget that these same talents are granted, once again, by Allah. Even if he sacrifices his life for the sake of Allah, he should think more of his failings than of the sacrifice made by him.

This acknowledgement of one's inability to do anything worthwhile in Allah's cause and his repentance are the very essence of all acts of worship and obedience. The Qur'ān identifies it as the spirit of humanness. The Qur'ān reproaches the hypocrites for their mistaken belief that they did a favour to Allah and His Messenger by embracing Islam. They are told that they have not done any favour. Rather, they should be grateful to Allah that He guided them to Islam.

How to develop modesty

Since modesty occupies such an important place in the Islamic scheme of things, let us study how to develop and train it. As already indicated, a proper understanding of divine attributes is instrumental in developing this virtue. We should therefore be constantly mindful of divine attributes – no easy task. Our memorization of divine names and their recital at certain hours cannot suffice. Such above practice may earn one some reward. However, it will not serve the purpose of embedding in us the virtue of modesty. Our whole outlook on life should be permeated with a sound perception of divine attributes, an essential requirement for self-development. This can be achieved only by reflecting upon the Qur'ān and the *Ḥadīth*, as these bring out clearly and fully the link between divine attributes and human life. It is therefore imperative to study deeply the Qur'ān and the *Hadīth*.

If a Muslim does not have the courage to himself wage *Jihād*, he should at least join the company of those who are committed to the ideal of *Jihād*. Good company is a great blessing, and it is most important to sustain it. Allah has promised His help to the seekers of truth on this count. Whoever resolves to pursue this way is promised all help and support by Allah, for He declares: 'We will open Our way for those who strive in Our cause.' (al-'Ankabūt 29:69)

Modesty is an important virtue. The Prophet's observations about it have been elaborated by the *'ulamā'*. That Allah is reluctant to turn down the supplication of those who are shy of Him is a great privilege. One who attains this rank can be regarded as a truly fortunate person.

Commitment

Commitment is another essential prerequisite of faith. It refers to the believer's resolve to fulfill the obligation which he owes to his Lord. Our relationship with Allah is based on two covenants. The first is the primordial covenant undertaken by the human spirit even before our birth, to which the following reference is made in the Qur'ānic passage: 'And recall when your Lord brought forth from the children of Adam their progeny from their backs and made them testify as to themselves, saying: "Am I not your Lord?" They said: "Yes! We testify." That was lest you should say on the Day of Resurrection: Of this we were unaware.' (al-A'rāf 7:172) This is called the natural covenant (*fiṭratallāh al-latī faṭara al-nās 'alayhā*) Establish Allah's handiwork according to the pattern on which He has made mankind; in the Qur'ān (al-Rūm 30:30).

Natural covenant

Included in this primordial covenant are the affirmation of monotheism and the discernment of right and wrong. Accordingly, Allah adduces the human self as an argument itself: 'By the soul, and the proportion and order given to it, and inspiration as to its wrong and its right. Surely blissful is he who has cleansed his soul, and miserable is he who has corrupted it.' (al-Shams 91:7-10)

With the help of this covenant a sensible person understands monotheism and moral value, and, in view of that understanding, will be held accountable for his beliefs and deeds, irrespective of whether the Messenger's call reached him or not. For the primordial covenant stands out as a weighty argument applicable to every human being. In the face of it, no one can plead his ignorance, a point emphasized in verse 172 of *al-A'rāf*. The Qur'ān holds that man remembers this covenant so vividly that his disobedience to Allah is tantamount to open defiance of Him (al-Qiyāmah 75:5). Man's conscience, as moral custodian, constantly reminds man of his covenant with Allah. He cannot suppress the voice of conscience: 'Man shall be an evidence against himself, though he may put forth pleas.' (al-Qiyāmah 75:14-15) He may at most plead forgetfulness, but he cannot silence the voice of conscience altogether. His conscience reproaches him for every evil act done by him. He may, through stubborn obduracy, disregard his conscience fully. However, we would emphasize that the inner voice does not stand in need of any argument or evidence; its existence is so consistently experienced that it cannot be denied. Kant describes it as something above and beyond philosophy, logic and argument – a wise observation.

That man instinctively distinguishes good and evil is commonplace. Although an individual may treat others unjustly, he himself takes offence at the same treatment from others and protests against it. This is clear proof that he is innately aware of good and evil. Misled by self-deception, however, he wrongs others while he desires that others should do good to him. The Qur'ān exposes this human weakness thus: 'Woe to those who deal in fraud, those who when they take from others, exact full measure, and when they measure to them or weigh for them, diminish.' (al-Muṭaffifīn 83:1-3)

Sharī'ah covenant

Although the primordial covenant is sufficient to hold man morally responsible, Allah did man another favour by sending down His Messengers and *Sharī'ah* to complete and elucidate this covenant. It is crystal clear to man that he should not deviate from the straight way. Man should rather act on reason and this argument holds true for everyone: 'He who was to perish might perish after an evidence and he who was to survive might survive after an evidence.' (al-Anfāl 8:42) It is evident that *Sharī'ah* is not something unnatural for man. It represents another covenant, which reiterates the primordial covenant. It puts an end to all error. In other words, *Sharī'ah* stands out as another clear light, besides the primordial covenant, to guide mankind. It illuminates him both outwardly and inwardly, as is stated in the following parable: 'Allah is the light of the heavens and the earth; the likeness of His light is as a niche wherein is a lamp; the lamp is in a glass; the glass is as though it is a star brilliant; lit from a tree blessed, an olive, neither of the east nor of the west; its very oil will shine forth, even though no fire touched it; light upon light!' (al-Nūr 24:35).

In the Qur'ān, *Sharī'ah* is referred to so frequently as the covenant that it is unnecessary to cite the relevant passages. Some *sūrahs* deal with the importance and responsibilities of this covenant, bringing home the truth that man's success in both the worlds is contingent upon his commitment to it. The Qur'ānic account gives a clear picture of man's role, duties and responsibilities. If he fulfills these, he will earn reward from Allah in both the worlds; if he violates the covenant, he will face punishment in both the worlds.

In one Qur'ānic passage the covenant is described as follows: 'And remember Allah's favour on you and His bond with which He bound you firmly when you said: "We hear and we obey." And fear Allah: surely Allah is the Knower of what is in your breast.' (al-Mā'idah 5:7) Allah's favour signifies the covenant or *Sharī'ah* which represents Allah's grace towards mankind. Man is obliged to obey the commands of *Sharī'ah* and fulfill the obligations arising out of the covenant. Since mankind pledged obedience to it, it is binding upon it. This covenant was made by the first members of the Muslim community – the Prophet's Companions who are the immediate addressees of the Qur'ān. This bond, nonetheless, applies in an equal measure to all of us. For we lay claim to follow in their footsteps. None of us would like to be deprived of the privilege conferred upon them.

Commitment

It is not an easy task to be true to both these covenants. It calls for hard work and true dedication to come up to the standard of faith and works required by these covenants. A believer is tested at every step. Only those blessed by Allah pass successfully through these tests. We should therefore be constantly mindful of these covenants. Performing certain rituals does not absolve us of our duty. Rather, our duty is obeying each and every command of Allah and His Messenger with total integrity and commitment, even though it may involve the sacrifice of one's life and wealth, family members and tribal ties. Earlier communities mistakenly held that their performance of certain rituals would include them among true believers. However, Allah does not accept those who pay only lip service to these covenants. This point comes out in the following Qur'ānic address directed at the Jews and Christians: 'Virtue is not in this that you turn your faces to the east and the west. Rather, virtue is of him who believes in Allah and the Last Day and the angels and the Book and the Prophet, and gives of his substance for love of Allah to kindred and orphans and the needy and the wayfarer and the beggar and for redeeming captives; and who establishes prayer and pays *zakāh* and is among the performers of their promises when they have promised; and is among the patient in adversity and affliction and in time of violence. These are they who affirm truth and these are they who are God-fearing.' (al-Baqarah 2:177)

Exegesis of a relevant verse

The passage just cited clarifies fully what is required by a true commitment to Allah. It is, therefore, pertinent that we study the passage at length and establish its meaning and message in the light of the Qur'ān itself.

Generally the expression '*birr*' is translated as 'virtue' or 'piety'. However, this does not bring out fully the import of the Qur'ān here. Commitment is a better alternative. For the term carries the connotations of obedience. It is used of a son who is dutiful to his parents and fulfills his obligations towards them. Likewise, it is employed in the context of Allah in order to signify that He will fulfill all His promises made to mankind. In the light of that we can see why commitment to Allah is not expressed merely by turning the face to the east or west. At best this represents only acknowledgement of a religious command. Only those are truly committed believers who have a firm conviction in Allah, the Day of Judgement, angels, the Book and the Messenger, and whose deeds are characterized by their generosity towards their relatives, towards orphans, the needy, travellers, beggars and slaves.

This point is made in a particular context. As already noted, the passage is addressed to the Jews and Christians who were engaged in a religious controversy about whether the direction of prayer lay to the east or the west. For them it was the most important issue, whereas they neglected their other obligations and requirements of faith. They are warned that such rituals do not signify their commitment to Allah. Only those will be taken as true believers who both practise and profess faith sincerely. Almost the same note of warning was addressed to the Jews by the Prophet Jesus (peace and blessings be upon him) when he criticized them for straining gnats while swallowing up camels. They were particular only about outward cleanliness while their souls were stained with major sins.

It is worth noting that spending generously in the cause of Allah is mentioned as a primary requirement of faith. Generally speaking, the Qur'ān accords pride of place to prayer. In this particular passage, however, it is mentioned later. It is equally significant that reference is made to both spending money in Allah's cause and to paying *zakāh*. One thus learns that a believer is obliged not only to pay *zakāh*, he is also charged with the responsibility of spending generously in Allah's cause. It is the obligation proceeding from his commitment to Allah.

Let us now turn to some other points implicit in the above Qur'ānic passage. As already indicated, spending in the cause of Allah is given precedence here over the prayer. In other Qur'ānic passages mention is made first of prayer. What accounts for this is that here it is being explained that a believer attains the proper degree of commitment by spending generously in the cause of Allah. The Muslim is elevated to higher ranks in the sight of Allah as he sacrifices what he holds dear in His cause. Almost the same argument recurs in verse 92 of *Āl 'Imrān* which pointedly declares that one cannot be taken as a sincere servant of Allah unless he spends what he holds dearest in Allah's cause. True believers are therefore defined as those who, notwithstanding their attachment to their possessions, spend them in Allah's cause. The love for possessions may rest on many factors. The possession may be something rare and precious, or it may be something of value especially in times of scarcity, that one is in need of oneself. However, when the believer prefers others to himself, he indicates his commitment to Allah. The same point is made in verse 9 of

Sūrah al-Ḥashr where those believers are commended who prefer others to themselves, notwithstanding their own neediness.

There is a question as to whether a Muslim is obliged to spend in addition to the obligation of *zakāh*. The answer is that the payment of *zakāh* is the minimum duty obligatory upon a Muslim; defaulters will be brought to book by the Islamic state. However, the state cannot prosecute those who pay *zakāh*. By contrast, Allah demands of believers both the payment of *zakāh* and spending in His cause openly as well as secretly. If the community is faced with calamity or is engaged in war, believers should spend generously in Allah's cause. It will be like a loan repayable by Allah in the Hereafter. The limit for such spending is also prescribed by the Qur'ān in suggesting that one should spend all that he has after meeting the needs of his family. This is the standard which true believers should follow. Allah blesses such committed believers with wisdom. And whoever is granted wisdom is immensely blessed (al-Baqarah 2:269).

The long verse cited earlier (2:177) characterizes true believers as those who are habitually true to their promise. Whenever they make a promise, they fulfill it faithfully. They put even their life at stake in keeping true to their word. Given this, it is naturally expected that they are most particular about the commitments they have made to Allah. The passage emphasizes also the quality of perseverance in true believers. Even in the face of poverty, starvation, physical suffering and afflictions caused by war they consistently discharge their obligations towards Allah.

To sum up: commitment is intrinsically linked with consistency. Faith demands both of these traits. Believers are expected to display utmost perseverance in professing and practising faith. While censuring the hypocrites Allah asks whether their verbal claim alone will help them to be counted among the believers. He will certainly put them to a test in order to ascertain the degree of their commitment. Allah does not accept the claim of every person. Only those gain nearness to Him who emerge successful in all the tests and trials and prove their integrity and obedience in respect of their covenant. Such will be reckoned as truthful by Allah, and in the Qur'ān they are called pious.

SENSITIVITY, SOLIDARITY AND *JIHĀD*

Solidarity and actual support and *jihād* are essential requirements of the faith, and in the cause of Allah an eloquent testimony of the believers' true faith. Those devoid of it cannot be considered sincere believers; indeed, those who claim faith and are lacking in solidarity can be regarded as no better than hypocrites.

It goes without saying that Allah does not stand in need of anyone's solidarity, help or support. He is independent in Himself. However, in matters of faith His dispensation is that He does not compel anyone to accept faith. He has granted everyone a choice in accepting or rejecting faith. If an individual exercises his choice to embrace the faith, and makes sacrifices in its cause, Allah appreciates his efforts and rewards him in both the worlds. As to those who reject true faith or those who despite their claim do not fulfill the obligations of faith, they suffer loss in both the worlds. According to the Qur'ān such people incur His wrath. Far from earning any reward from Allah, they are afflicted with His displeasure.

In view of this definition of faith, it is essential that we devote ourselves fully to His faith and strive for upholding it. Allah loves those who have a strong attachment to their faith. Notwithstanding His being Independent He loves those servants who express their utmost devotion to faith. Solidarity, support and *jihād* are the steady manifestations of this devotion. These are closely interrelated. Let us discuss each of these separately.

Sensitivity

A person with a strong faith is characterized by sensitivity for it. He does not behave like a mute spectator to injustice, victimization and to the conflict between truth and falsehood. He is bound to help the victims of injustice to the extent of his capacity, and to resist and restrain the oppressor, even at the risk of his own life. Those who do not respond thus are devoid of the essential qualities of manliness. It is illustrated best by the Prophet Moses's conduct. When he saw a weak Israelite being beaten up by a Copt, he did not pass by. Rather, he immediately came to the rescue of the victim. As the oppressor died at his hands, without his intending that, he deeply regretted the incident and repented sincerely for the killing. His only goal had been to help the victim; he had not been prompted by any desire to kill the oppressor. Solidarity, especially when it is motivated by familial or tribal or ethnic loyalties motives, may fail to discriminate between truth and falsehood. However, if sincere in his faith, a believer does not commit any excess. As already indicated, the Prophet Moses (peace and blessings be upon him) copiously regretted the unintended consequence of his action and Allah accepted his repentance. A similar incident happened the next day. When the Prophet Moses (peace and blessings be upon him) came out, he found the same Israelite quarrelling with another Copt. He was again moved by what he saw but, this time, his response was different. He realized that the fellow Israelite appeared to be a quarrelsome individual and he therefore proceeded to restrain him from committing any evil. Dissuading him from evil was another manifestation of the same feeling of solidarity. This point is often disregarded. The Prophet Muḥammad (peace and blessings be upon him) said: 'Help your brother, be he the oppressor or the oppressed.' When asked how one would help the oppressor, he clarified that restraining him from committing injustice amounts to helping him. (Bukhārī and Muslim)

The Prophet Moses (peace and blessings be upon him) intended to help his fellow Israelite in the latter form. However, when the Israelite saw him approaching and, holding him to be in the wrong, he feared punishment at his hands. He therefore exclaimed: 'As you killed a Copt yesterday, you intend to kill me today.' This he followed up with the wicked comment: 'You pretend to be a reformer, but you act as a transgressor.' The Israelite thus divulged the killing of the Copt by the Prophet Moses (peace and blessings be upon him) who had to leave Egypt in order to escape Pharaoh's punishment. This appears to have been the heavy price for his act of solidarity since it forced him into exile. Those blessed by Allah make many such, indeed greater, sacrifices in the cause, even laying down all that what they have.

A similar trial was faced by the Prophet Moses (peace and blessings be upon him) on reaching Madyan. When he arrived there, he sat beside a well. He did not know where to go and what to do. In such a situation one is totally lost in his own predicament and does not think of the plight of others. However, he acted differently even in such a difficult situation. He noted that shepherds were watering their goats while two girls stood at a distance along with their herd. He felt pity for them and asked why they waited so long. They explained that since their father was an old person, they had to look after their goats and they found it hard to water their animals while the men were around, and had to wait until the others had left. On hearing this, he came to their rescue, offered to water their herd, and then returned to his place. He did not say a word about his own predicament. However, he kept on invoking Allah: 'O Lord! I have need of whatever good You send me.' (al-Qaṣaṣ 28:24) A little later he realized that this indeed was his destination. He had suffered on account of displaying solidarity in the cause of truth. This, however, helped him find his destination. Allah alone can reward one in this way; especially those who are righteous and pious in nature. Such persons undergo many trials but pass them successfully. This is a truth that is little recognized. The Prophet's directive is: 'If you see anything opposed to *Sharīʿah* and are in a position to rectify it, you should do so. If you do not have such authority, you should resist it verbally. If you are not able to do even this much you should resent it in your heart and this is the lowest degree of faith.' (Ibn Mājah) The concluding words of this *ḥadīth* are worth noting. One who does not resist an act opposed to the *Sharīʿah* even in his heart, and does not shun it in his individual capacity, his faith is less than the lowest degree of faith. Allah directs the believers to move away from social gatherings in which divine symbols and commands are disrespected: 'Do not join the company of those who reject and mock divine signs.' (al-Nisā' 4:140) Far from cultivating such people if a believer ever falls in with them by mistake, he should immediately quit their company as he recalls the divine directive. Allah describes such people as those who wrong their own souls. The Qur'ān therefore insists that the believers should not join their company when they remember the divine directive (al-Anʿām 6:68).

Two points emerge clearly from the foregoing discussion: (1) A believer cannot associate with those who are disrespectful towards Allah's faith except by error or, if deliberately, for the purpose of reforming them. (2) If he knowingly joins their company, he is to be considered as one of them and will be recompensed with them.

We learn from a *ḥadīth* that Allah once directed angels to overturn a particular town. The angels submitted that a pious servant of Allah lived in that town. Nevertheless, they were commanded to destroy it. For that pious person did not protest against the sacrilege committed in that town. Here is the relevant *ḥadīth*: 'It is reported on the authority of Jābir that the Prophet (peace and blessings be upon him) said: Allah directed Gabriel to destroy a particular town along with all its inhabitants. Gabriel submitted: "There lives a pious servant of Yours who never disobeyed You." He was commanded: "Destroy every one of them. For even that person did not protest against the disrespect shown to My faith."' It is clear that Allah does not attach any importance to rituals, especially the ones performed by those who are not genuinely attached to true faith. Allah is earnestly concerned in matters of faith and does not accept some superficial rituals in the name of faith.

Solidarity

Solidarity for a cause demands that one should come out openly in support of it. It is a measure of one's level of commitment. Knowing it is essential so that the worth of the individual's commitment to faith can be reckoned. Commitment to faith is the real thing, while other considerations are peripheral. An individual may be endowed with wealth, family ties, sound health, physical power and knowledge. However, if he lacks concern for the faith, his possessions and qualities are worthless. By contrast, a resourceless person abounding in love for the faith is a valuable asset of the community – he will be found at the head of the army defending the cause of faith.

In view of the central importance of solidarity, Allah regards it as the criterion of the genuineness of one's faith. A true believer is expected to sacrifice his life and wealth in the cause of truth – his ultimate success or failure depends upon such sacrifice. Whoever passes this test is a genuine believer, and those who fail it are mere hypocrites.

The Qur'ān makes it plain that Allah is not dependent upon anyone to defend truth. He is perfectly capable of establishing and vindicating truth. However, in His infinite wisdom He has decided that man be given a free choice in order to test who sacrifices his life and possessions in His cause and who opposes Him. This truth is articulated thus in the Qur'ān: 'And had Allah willed, He would have vindicated Himself against them. But He ordained fighting so that He may test you one by the other.' (Muḥammad 47:4) The command to Muslims to fight against the unbelievers and polytheists does not rest on the consideration that Allah stands in need of the believers to reinforce His faith.

He is perfectly independent and omnipotent. It is, nonetheless, part of His grand design that the sincere believers and hypocrites be tested, and the former one helped and supported by Him.

Allah has subjected the believers to this test so that they may help His cause. He promises to help those who do: 'Surely Allah shall aid him who aids His cause. Surely Allah is Strong, Mighty.' (al-Ḥajj 22:40) One learns from this verse that in urging the believers to help His cause, Allah enables divine support to reach those who strive to establish the true faith. The Messenger is an evident manifestation of this support. Any help to the Messenger is help to the One who sent him: 'There comes to you a Messenger confirming what is with you; you shall surely believe in him and help him.' (Āl 'Imrān 3:81) Help and support to the Messenger entitles the following reward: 'Those who believe in him and honour him and help him and follow the light which has been sent down with him, those are the prosperous.' (al-A'rāf 7:157)

Muslims should also help and support each other. In fact, since they represent a fraternity, this is an obligation. If a Muslim seeks help from a fellow Muslim in matters of faith, the latter is obliged to help him to the extent of his capacity. If he fails in his duty, notwithstanding his resources, he will be reproached in this life and will be held answerable in the Hereafter. In the early phase of Islamic faith, this directive assumed special significance. Some of the early Muslims were directed to emigrate to such places where they could practise their faith in safety. Other Muslims were directed to help the emigrants so that they could sustain themselves. The emigrants were entitled to help from their fellow Muslims, specially in defending their faith. So too were those who could not, for particular reasons, emigrate to safety: Allah says: 'And should they seek succour from you in the matter of religion, then incumbent upon you is their succour.' (al-Anfāl 8:72) This duty is binding in Islam. It can be disregarded only on the basis of some genuine grounds which are stated in the Qur'ān. Otherwise, every Muslim is obliged to discharge this duty.

Jihād

In terms of commitment to faith, and support and help for it, the final stage is represented by *Jihād*. At times, the situation demands that the pious servants of Allah organize themselves and provide resources needed to withstand dangers and remove obstacles to the faith. Obviously such danger cannot be averted by individuals acting separately. As the danger is faced by the entire community, all its members are obliged to fight against it. Truth is undoubtedly an important force with tremendous appeal. Yet Allah has charged His pious servants with the responsibility of defending His faith with force when circumstances compel it. The law of survival demands that the believers come out openly in help and support of their faith.

It is on record that the Prophet Jesus (peace and blessings be upon him) exhorted his disciples to wage *Jihād*. The same call was given by all the Messengers. We have made special mention of the Prophet Jesus (peace and blessings be upon him) in this context for two reasons. First, it is generally held that his mission consisted only of sermons and advice and that he did not urge his followers to wage *Jihād*. The second reason is that the Qur'ān cites his response as the role model for Muslims. The Qur'ānic account is as follows: 'O believers! Be Allah's helpers, even as Jesus, son of Maryam, said to the disciples: "Who shall be my helpers for Allah?" The disciples said: "We are Allah's helpers." Then a party of the Children of Israel believed, and another party disbelieved. Then We strengthened those who believed against their foe; so they became triumphant.' (al-Ṣaff 61:14); see also in *Sūrah Āl 'Imrān* (3:52). One thus recognizes that in line with the practice of earlier Messengers the Prophet Jesus (peace and blessings be upon him) first asked the leading members of his community to respond positively to his call. However, as he realized that they were unrelenting in their opposition to faith, he turned to the poor members of his community, urging them to follow him. The latter accepted this call and they were instrumental in spreading his mission. The Qur'ān brings out the truth thus: 'When Jesus perceived unbelief in them, he said: "Who will be my helpers for Allah?" The disciples said: "We are helpers of Allah. We believe in Allah, and bear you witness that surely we are Muslims."' (Āl 'Imrān 3:52)

The above verse is relevant in this context for the point we made earlier that believers are instinctively committed to faith. Allah blesses with such commitment those who preserve their integrity, irrespective of whether they are rich or poor, prominent or lowly members of their community. The Prophet Jesus (peace and blessings be upon him) was fully conversant with this truth. As he realized that the leading members of his community were not interested in truth, he turned to the poor members of the community. Allah blessed them in that they rose to be the champions of truth and guided all of mankind. Although they were ordinary fishermen, they prevailed over earthly kings.

The role model presented by the Prophet Jesus's disciples was re-enacted most effectively by the *Anṣār* of Madina in expressing their commitment to truth and the spirit of *Jihād*. Reports indicate that the *Anṣār* were profoundly impressed by the Prophet Muḥammad's conduct when they visited Makka for *Ḥajj*. They learnt about his call to virtue and faith. They noted also that the Makkans were opposed to him and did not pay any heed to truth. It evoked among the *Anṣār* of Madina their commitment to truth and some of them readily expressed their desire to stand up for it. They communicated the Prophet's call to their friends and family members in Madina. Soon Islam was established firmly in Madina. The persecuted Muslims of Makka took Madina as their refuge and began emigrating there. It was first the poor Muslims who emigrated to Madina. At a later stage, Allah ordered the Prophet Muḥammad (peace and blessings be upon him) to emigrate as well. Later on, Madina naturally became the 'capital' of Islam.

The *Anṣār* warmly and generously welcomed the *Muhājirūn*, making them partners in their property, farmhouses and orchards. Likewise, they treated the Prophet (peace and blessings be upon him) with the utmost respect and love. Their commitment in this regard is unprecedented in history. As well as the moral bond of fraternity, the relationship between the *Anṣār* (Helpers) and the *Muhājirūn* (Immigrants) for a time had a legal standing. It was not the *Anṣār* who revoked its legal status. Rather, in line with *Sharī'ah* commands and the spirit of Islamic law, this brotherhood was divested of its legal character. Once the *Muhājirūn* had become settled and integrated into Madinan society, it was no longer necessary that they be provided with some extra protection.

It must be added that the *Anṣār* were not motivated economically or politically in granting refuge and space to the *Muhājirūn*. On the contrary, they generously made the Makkans partners in their economic pursuits, though the latter had been left utterly resourceless by the persecution of the unbelieving Quraysh. Politically it was a major blunder in that in turning Madina into the headquarters of Islam they provoked the hostility of both the Arab and the non-Arab states. The *Anṣār* were not unaware of the implications of their decision. On the contrary, they understood full well the dangers and risks in embracing Islam. The Quraysh had alerted them against the dangers. Reports suggest that when the Quraysh realized that the *Anṣār* intended to invite the Prophet (peace and blessings be upon him) to Madina, they openly warned that this action of theirs would engender war on a massive scale. However, the *Anṣār* paid no attention to these warnings and threats.

After the Prophet's emigration to Madina, there ensued a series of attacks on Madina. Yet it did not deter or demoralize the *Anṣār*. They consistently fulfilled their obligations to the Prophet (peace and blessings be upon him). Before certain battles, when they sensed that the Prophet (peace and blessings be upon him) needed to know about their response and resilience, their leaders assured the Prophet (peace and blessings be upon him) in no uncertain terms of their total help and support. On one such occasion an *Anṣār* leader proclaimed: 'O Messenger of Allah! Unlike the children of Israel we will never tell you to wage war on your own while we sit back in our homes. By Allah! If you ask us to jump into the sea along with our horses we will obey this command without questioning it.'

MAN'S RELATIONSHIP WITH HIS OWN SELF

In the preceding chapters we have tried to bring out some of the implications of man's relationship with Allah. In the light of that discussion it is easier to figure out man's relationship with his own self. A Muslim readily affirms that he is not the creator of himself; he affirms that he is a servant of Allah. Given this he cannot claim absolute freedom and sovereignty over himself. He is morally bound by the knowledge that all his actions should be in line with the will and pleasure of his creator. For it is Allah Who has granted life to man and sustains him in every respect. In the light of this perception we realize that all our faculties and potentials are a trust assigned to us by our Lord. We should act honestly and justly with the trust placed in us. We are not free to destroy or abuse any of these faculties and potentials. Nor can we sell or pawn them, or employ them in a manner not approved by Allah.

Allah has blessed man with the balance of faculties essential for his existence and survival. None of these is superfluous, so that it may be discarded. It is man who abuses his faculties for evil purposes, his faculties and talents are not evil in themselves. If he uses these properly, they will serve him and his fellow human beings. If he abuses them, he will incur loss in both the worlds. An example of imbalance and abuse is monks and ascetics who mistakenly hold the body and physical faculties to be an obstacle to the growth of the spirit and accordingly afflict themselves with strenuous physical disciplines. Far from attaining the goal of developing their soul and spirit, they harm themselves irreparably by denying the body its due. The human soul is sustained by material objects in this world. If the body grows properly, it strengthens the soul. By contrast, a diseased body suffers from a weak soul. Let us illustrate the point further. Ascetics misconstrue sexual desire as something fatal and believe that it must be suppressed for spiritual growth and self-purification. In fact, one who lack's desire may become devoid of manly strength and courage. Without these qualities he only leads a partial life. At most he may develop some mystic traits and qualify as a religious-minded person. However, he cannot achieve any manly and chivalrous deed.

We have mentioned this warning because, under the influence of the fallacious mystical concept, even some Muslim Sufi masters have prescribed disciplines not endorsed by *Sharī'ah*, and insisted on them. They suppose that the hardships involved in these disciplines elevate the human spirit. Not only do they eat and drink very little, they go so far as to try and abandon food and drink altogether. They suffer from the delusion that this enlightens the self, in a way enabling it to perceive even the unseen.

Such notions cannot be traced back to the Prophet (peace and blessings be upon him) and his Companions. They enjoyed such perfect spiritual mastery, as cannot be equalled, yet they professed and practised moderation and balance. The Prophet (peace and blessings be upon him) checked any extremist tendency on the part of his Companions. He warned them against any imbalance in matters of faith. He declared: 'Whoever tries to practice extremism in faith will be humbled.'

Some held that it was contrary to faith to enjoy any worldly bounty and expressed their desire to renounce life. Upon hearing this, the Prophet (peace and blessings be upon him) told them: 'Among you I am the one blessed with the best knowledge, and I am the most fearful of Allah. How can you avoid the acts which

I perform?' It is reported on the authority of Umm al-Mu'minīn 'Ā'ishah that when the Prophet (peace and blessings be upon him) granted allowance in certain matters, it was noticed that some were reluctant to avail themselves of this allowance. He gathered them together and told them: 'What is it with some people that they avoid what I unhesitatingly do? By Allah! I know Allah better than they do and I fear Him more than them.' (Bukhārī) This truth is clear also from another *ḥadīth*, cited by Anas: 'The Prophet (peace and blessings be upon him) used to say: "Do not be extremist otherwise Allah will treat you harshly. A community was harsh upon itself. As a result Allah let all harshness be directed towards them. You can see these practices in monasteries and convents."' (Abū Dā'ūd).

As to those who held that the body be suppressed to attain spiritual progress, the Prophet (peace and blessings be upon him) directed that they owed certain obligations to their body. In the following report he refers to certain demands of the body. 'Abdullāh ibn 'Umar reports: 'Once the Prophet (peace and blessings be upon him) asked me whether it was true that I fasted in the day-time and offered prayers throughout the night. When I affirmed this, he told me: "Do not do so. You should fast at times and not do so on other days. You should pray and sleep as well. For your body owes certain rights over you. Your wife has her rights upon you. So do your visitors and guests have their rights upon you." (Bukhārī)

These *aḥādīth* present to us the real spirit of Islam. We learn that Islam does not ask man to blunt any of his natural faculties and potentials for spiritual growth. Rather, it directs him to act with moderation and utilize his potentials in the right proportion and direction. Islam provides ample guidance about the proper utilization. It prescribes also how to control one's base desires and how to pursue the straight way steadily. However, those who want to make a show of their religiosity are not content with the teachings of Allah and His Messenger. They alter Islamic teachings in order to draw attention to themselves, and claim to be more religious. They are apt to disregard the teachings of faith and focus only on their innovations. This culminates in the abolition of the *Sunnah* as innovations gain currency. The Prophet (peace and blessings be upon him) rightly held that an innovation in matters of faith is always at the expense of abolishing the *Sunnah*.

Obligations towards the self

There are many misconceptions about the human self. Some Sufi masters appear to have made the same mistakes as were made earlier by Christian monks. They were influenced also by Hindu spiritual masters. It is therefore imperative to ascertain one's obligations towards the self and learn how to fulfill these in the light of the Qur'ān and the *Ḥadīth*.

The first obligation – quest for truth

The first and foremost duty of man is to gain a true and complete understanding of his self. Man represents a microcosm and his self is endowed with the knowledge which is necessary for leading life. Earlier the wise men of ancient times were cognizant of this truth. Socrates is reported to have said that man should first know himself. This point was amplified by Plato who argued that the

208

human soul knows the truth before its descent into the world, but man is apt to be forgetful and needs to be reminded of the reality. Aristotle expressed the view that if man discovers his potentials, it would suffice for him. Similar views have also been expressed on this subject by the eminent philosophers and thinkers of other traditions.

The Qur'ān makes it plain that prior to man's descent to the world Allah made all the souls of human beings testify to His Oneness and Lordship: 'And recall when your Lord brought forth from the children of Adam their progeny from their backs and made them testify as to themselves, saying: Am I not your Lord? They said: Yes.' (al-A'rāf 7:172) The Qur'ān further clarifies that Allah has created the human self so that man instinctively discerns between good and evil. This leaves no room whatever for man to plead his ignorance: 'By the soul and the order and proportion given to it, and inspiration as to its wrong and right.' (al-Shams 91:7-8) The Qur'ān affirms that man is a witness unto himself, notwithstanding his resorting to various pretexts: 'Nay! Man shall be an evidence against himself, though he may put forth pleas.' (al-Qiyāmah 75:14-15).

The Qur'ān establishes that Allah has devised an elaborate arrangement for man's guidance. The first and foremost point is that He has blessed man with a true understanding of his own self. Furthermore, He has instructed man through His revelation, which enlightens man sufficiently. Let us add that those who seek the truth are readily guided by divine revelation. In contrast, those indifferent to guidance grope and wander in darkness and ignorance. It is therefore imperative that man take cognizance of his immense potential, take stock of himself and try to draw upon his faculties and potentials. The inner voice is the most effective means for guiding man. The more one listens to it, the more guided one becomes. This does not call for any further proof or evidence. It is a weighty argument in itself.

The second obligation – training the self

Man is under an obligation to train his self. This means is that he should take every possible step to make use of the light provided by Allah for his guidance. Indeed, he should constantly strive to strengthen and enhance this light. This consists in his being watchful. He should be guided by divine light and respond to its demands. His conscience never falters in guiding him. However, at times, under the influence of base desires, he may resort to pretexts to silence his conscience. If this becomes habitual, his conscience grows weaker and ultimately atrophies. At this point he cannot derive any guidance and he is totally deprived of the inner light.

To protect himself against this disaster it is essential that he should not oppose his conscience, nor shy away from making the highest sacrifice in this cause. He should never become reconciled to failure of conscience. For a person with a dead conscience leads a cursed life on earth. If guilty of this and yet concerned to revive his spiritual life, he should openly confess himself before his Creator and resolve firmly not to commit sin again.

As to the goal of training the self, one should follow the way prescribed by Allah. This way differs sharply from the one prescribed by certain Sufi masters who, swayed by their pantheistic vision, considered some form of union with the divine as the highest point imaginable for the human self. However, we reject this proposition as no more than a flight of fancy. According to the Qur'ān, the highest stage for the human self is to develop a contentment that will help him earn Allah's pleasure in the Hereafter: 'O soul at peace! Return unto your Lord, well-pleased and well-pleasing.' (al-Fajr 89:27-28)

The contented or peaceful soul represents that quality of conviction that is not shaken even in the face of the most difficult trials. His attaining Allah's pleasure consists in his realization of all his expectations with Allah. This is the highest rank imaginable for man. It is this that entitles him to enter Paradise (al-Fajr 89: 29-30). Even though he may not have seen this glad tiding in a dream, he will achieve this rank. In contrast, those with some allegedly supernatural power that enables them to walk on water or fly in the air will not attain success in the Hereafter.

The foregoing gives a clear picture of the ideal training of the self. It is an arduous task, which calls for guidance at every step. This may be achieved with the help of studying the Qur'ān and emulating the role model of the Companions. However, study of the Qur'ān must be done with an open and critical mind, as well as the conviction that only the Messengers possess perfect knowledge.

The third obligation – self respect

Man owes another obligation to his self – of respecting it. This does not mean having delusions of importance or grandeur. Those afflicted with arrogance are deluded by Satan and are bound to suffer losses. What is meant by self-respect is that man should constantly remember that he has been honoured with the vicegerency on earth and that Allah has made him trustee of a burden which could not be shouldered by the heavens and the earth: 'We offered the trust to the heavens and the earth and the mountains. But they declined to bear it and shrank from it. But man undertook it.' (al-Aḥzāb 33:72)

Man has been blessed with potentials and faculties not granted to any other creature. Allah has made everything in the universe subservient to man while he is not subservient to any in the universe. Rather, Allah has selected man exclusively for subservience to Him. This elevated position demands that man not commit any act that may bring disgrace upon him. Since man occupies a high position, he is liable to a mighty fall. It is explained in a variety of ways in the Qur'ān that if man does not appreciate the honour bestowed upon him, he is relegated as the worst of creatures: 'Assuredly We have created man in the best mould. Thereafter We revert him to the lowest of the low.' (al-Tīn 95:4-5)

While recounting the history of the Jews the Qur'ān points out that Allah had granted them the leadership of mankind. However, they did not do justice to this privileged position. They were warned and still they did not take heed. As a result, Allah debased them and they fell to the lowest level. The Qur'ānic image is that of a dog who lolls out its tongue whether you strike it or spare it: 'And recite to them the story of the one to whom We gave Our signs, but he passed them by: so Satan followed him and he became of the perverted. And had We willed, We would surely have lifted him thereby, but he clung to the earth and pursued his desire, so his parable is the parable of a dog, who if you assail him lolls out his tongue and if you leave him alone then also lolls out his tongue. Such is the parable of the people who belie Our signs.' (al-Aʿrāf 7:175-176)

Man should recognize these truths with regard to self-respect. Otherwise he is vulnerable to Satan's mischief. Once man is overcome by Satan, Allah leaves him in that disgrace. It is perhaps needless to add that one disgraced by Allah cannot attain any honour (al-Ḥajj 22:18).

It is a point of the highest importance that one who does not have any self-respect is not respected by others. In other words, if he does not rate his faculties and potentials highly, but regards them as mere saleable commodities, he is guilty of not respecting his self. We should be careful about our goals, about whether these goals are consistent with divine teachings. If we do not take sufficient care in this respect, if we surrender to everyone, do not check our desires, and are apt to praise everyone, we cannot earn any respect.

The fourth obligation – self evaluation

It is essential that man constantly engage in soul-searching and stock-taking in terms of good and bad deeds done by him. For on this depends his deliverance in the Hereafter. Nothing will avail him except his deeds. On the basis of his deeds will he be punished or rewarded. Since he is accountable for every deed, however minor it might be, it is right that he call himself to account before he is held accountable before Allah. ʿUmar made the following insightful observation: 'Search your own self before you are called to account. Get ready for the Grand Assembly. They will have an easy reckoning on the Day of Judgement who engage in stock-taking.' (Tirmidhī) 'Umar is here elaborating the import of verse 18 of *Sūrah al-Ḥashr*.

The believer should continually take stock of his conduct. He may conveniently do so before he retires to sleep. However, the best time for it is a little before *fajr* when one offers *tahajjud* prayers. One is more likely to be blessed with divine mercy at this hour. He should not be lax or lenient in this stock-taking, nor make excuses or allowances for himself. On the contrary, when reviewing everything he should try to compensate for his every lapse and mistake. His repentance may help offset his obligations to Allah. However, the obligations that he owes to fellow human beings involve more difficulties. He should therefore try to make up for any wrong done by him. He should try to please those he has wronged, as well as seeking forgiveness from Allah for the excesses committed by him.

Index